Learning Centers in Kindergarten

by
Karen L. Loman
and
Dorothy P. Hall

(With help from Michelle S. Hall, a Pre-Kindergarten teacher)

Carson-Dellosa Publishing Company, Inc.
Greensboro, NC

Credits

Editor
Joey Bland

Cover Illustration
Dan Sharp

Cover Design
Annette Hollister-Papp

Layout Design
Jon Nawrocik

Inside Illustrations
Ray Lambert
Mike Duggins

ISBN 0-88724-211-1

Dedication

My friend and mentor Pat Cunningham describes a good kindergarten classroom as a literate home simulation. In other words, some children are lucky enough to come from homes where books are not only present, but are read to children daily. From these early experiences with books and reading, they profit from their instruction in school. Karen and I are fortunate to have come from two such homes and want to dedicate this book to our **mothers** who were responsible for this.

To my mother, **Jeanne Anita Mathieu Parzyk**, who shared her love of books and reading with her five daughters; I was fortunate to be one of them. Thank you for the wonderful start you gave me on the road to literacy!

> Dorothy (what my mother calls me, not Dottie as my friends do)

To my mother, **Jurhee Bench**, for her tireless efforts to nurture my childhood thirst for reading. I appreciate you and Dad for your steadfast support in everything I have ever done.

> Karen

Special Thanks

With thanks and appreciation to Dottie's daughter, **Michelle S. Hall** and her friend and colleague **Julie Curtis**, who teach pre-kindergarten in the Bright Beginnings Program at Plaza Road Pre-Kindergarten, a Title I school in Charlotte, NC. Michelle and Julie read our work, commented, and made sure the differences in pre-kindergarten and kindergarten were noted.

Table of Contents

Reading | Writing | Home Living | Community | Blocks | Science | Math | Art

Table of Contents

Reading | Writing | Home Living | Community | Blocks | Science | Math | Art

Introduction

Reading | Writing | Home Living | Community | Blocks | Science | Math | Art

Kindergarten has long been part of the school system in the United States and around the world. However, in some states and countries, kindergarten has only been publicly funded for the past few decades. Kindergarten is not usually mandated; many states set the compulsory age of school attendance at six or seven years old and the entrance age for kindergarten children is usually five years old. There are different cut-off dates for starting kindergarten and first grade, depending on where the child lives. Most children, no matter where they live, start school as soon as they are old enough to do so. Many school systems are finding that pre-kindergarten, or four-year-old kindergarten, is helpful for those young children who have had limited literacy experiences.

What kind of program is best for four- and five-year-olds? Obviously, one that is best adapted to the needs of its children. The five-year-old is learning rapidly. He wants to find out about things. He investigates, examines, and questions. If the children are only four years old, the program selected and the methods used must be adapted to the developmental needs of four-year-olds. If most of the children are older, either mentally or chronologically, then the activities need to be scaled to meet their needs.

Kindergarten was once a place where young children could begin school, learn, and "play" in a secure environment. Socio-emotional development was emphasized. As the idea of kindergarten expanded, schools began to feel responsible for academic development of these children. Kindergarten curriculums were developed in many schools and school systems. Often the goal of these curriculums is to get these young children as far as possible, as soon as possible in their academic development. In the zeal to establish a curriculum, emphasis is sometimes placed on cognitive development, and the important areas of emotional, social, and physical development are overshadowed. The relationship of child-initiated, exploratory activity to cognitive development is de-emphasized. If we look at the kindergarten model from 40 years ago in Foster and Headley's *Education in the Kindergarten* (American Book Company, 1959), the emphasis was not on literacy (reading and writing) but on the complete development of kindergarten children.

The past few decades have taught educators much about how young children learn to read and write. We know that literacy emerges from birth in young children who have experiences with words, books, and print. We also know that we can begin these activities in kindergarten and before. It is how we introduce these experiences that is as important as what we introduce in kindergarten. Learning Centers can play an important part in teaching the whole child.

Kindergarten classrooms have always been known for learning centers (once called the "work period")—places where children could learn as they "play." Learning centers—the Reading Center, Writing Center, Home Living Center or Dress Up Center, Art Center, Math Center, Science Center, Blocks Center, Puzzles Center, Sand and Water, Center, etc.—are an important part of literacy learning today and an important part of a developmentally appropriate kindergarten. It is in these learning centers that children explore and discover their environment individually or in small groups. In kindergarten, learning centers provide young children with opportunities to make choices and to self-manage and work together as they learn.

- For pre-kindergarten students, centers are their program. The children spend the whole day working or exploring their environment and learning in the centers in the classroom. This is often called the children's "work time." When the teacher reads to the class or works with the whole group or the big group, it is in the "Circle Time Center." After the big group meets here, the children often return to this "center" to imitate the teacher/student interactions during "work time." This offers the teacher a wonderful opportunity to observe their behavior and see if the students are picking up concepts introduced to the class.

- In Four-Blocks and other first-grade classrooms, centers are often used to enhance the language arts period and provide some additional help to students either one-on-one or in a small group. The Four-Blocks® Framework has many variations but there are two basic principles that must be followed if reading and writing instruction can truly be called Four Blocks. The first principle is the belief that children learn to read in different ways. Because of this belief each of the Four Blocks gets 30-40 minutes of instruction each and every day. Providing enough and equal time to each block assures that children are given the same opportunity to become literate regardless of which approach is most compatible with their individual learning personalities. The second basic principle is that, while we don't put children in fixed-ability groups, we make our instruction as multilevel as possible so that average, struggling and excelling students all learn to read and write at the highest possible level. Doing the Four Blocks every day and giving them approximately equal time is a simple matter of making a schedule and sticking to it. So, Four-Blocks teachers don't teach some children during one block and let the other children work independently in centers. But they do add an extra 30-45 minutes to the Four-Blocks schedule, if they have the time, and do some one-on-one and small group coaching during center time.

In kindergarten classes, the teacher plans the activities for each of the centers. The teacher decides what activities will help children learn more about a topic or theme they are studying in school or any area the children want or need to learn more about. Five-year-olds need to be provided with many hands-on activities because they learn by doing and by using all of their senses. The opportunity to verbalize and interact with other students and adults helps them internalize what they learn. Finally, the children should be in a risk-free environment, where they are encouraged to try new things without fear of failure, and where self-esteem is raised through a series of successful experiences.

The purpose of this book is to emphasize that learning centers are an important part of a developmentally appropriate kindergarten and an important part of the Building-Blocks™ Framework. In this book, we offer kindergarten teachers some ideas for center time and how to best adapt these ideas to pre-kindergarten and first grade Four-Blocks classes. If the ideas in this book are new to you, get ready to take some calculated risks. You will be delighted with the reactions of the young children you teach!

What Are Learning Centers?

Learning centers are designated areas within the classroom where children explore, construct, and play with materials. The teacher selects the materials and designs open-ended activities from which children choose. The teacher decides what the children will learn, then offers them a number of ways to explore and learn. From the variety of activities, the teacher and young children themselves learn what works best for each individual.

Young children learn and grow through play. Play is the primary means by which the child reconciles the reality of the world with his personal experiences. Activities within each learning center should accommodate this with multi-level experiences, multi-material opportunities, and occasions for interactions with others (Singer and Reverson, 1978). The activities within each center should enhance children's cognitive and social development, self-regulation, and curiosity. Cognitive development is promoted through the construction of knowledge with hands-on materials and experiences. Social development occurs through the interaction of the child with other children and the adults in the environment. Self-regulation is a result of the child making choices and following through with commitments and decisions. Curiosity is enhanced by true exploration of open-ended activities and materials. According to the National Association for the Education of Young Children (Bredekamp, ed., 1987) children need to:

- explore;
- develop the disposition to apply the knowledge and skills they have acquired;
- learn to self-manage;
- learn to work together; and
- express themselves in many different ways.

Young children do not come to kindergarten knowing what to do in each learning center or how to do it. How the centers are set up and interaction with an adult during center time is often critical to student development. Cognitive development results from exploring, talking, and sharing with a more knowledgeable person. Children learn through problem-solving experiences observed by and shared with someone else, usually a parent or teacher, but sometimes a sibling or peer. Often a parent, peer, or teacher can show the child what to do, support her first attempts, then let the child "work" independently. Adults can provide this scaffolding and encourage children to identify and solve problems they may not be capable of on their own without this initial help (www.Funderstanding.com). Children in literacy-enriched learning centers, with adult guidance and support, participate in more literacy behaviors during free time than children in thematic centers without adult guidance (Morrow and Rand cited in NREL, 1998).

Learning centers should allow for children to be actively involved in learning and making choices. Learning centers, along with whole group instruction and individual activities, comprise a balanced approach to early childhood instruction.

Learning Centers allow:

- teachers to practice curriculum integration.

- teachers to build on the current interests of children.

- individual or small groups of children to work and play cooperatively or alone.

- children to self-select activities and materials.

- children to use concrete, real, and relevant learning materials and activities.

- teachers to flexibly use a variety of work places and spaces.

- children to expand their abilities to communicate orally and through reading and writing and to enjoy these activities.

- the teacher to interact with individual or small groups of children within a center.

Opportunities to play, construct, and explore allow children to take risks, explore roles, make connections between the known and the new, solve problems, and engage in meaningful conversations (Owocki, 1999). Learning centers offer children the freedom and resources to build, role-play, and experiment with materials that are interesting to them in their own ways and in their own time.

In a Building-Blocks classroom, literacy is a primary focus of instruction. In kindergartens where literacy is the primary focus of the curriculum, books and something to write with and on, should be offered in every center. Each learning center should provide children opportunities to explore real reasons for reading and writing (Neuman and Roskos, 1997). For example, in the Blocks Center, children should have access to books on building and paper for drawing the structures they make. In the Home Living Center, children should use cookbooks, phone books, message pads, grocery lists, etc. In the Science Center, when studying a season, animals, or the weather, books on the topics are available in the center so that the children have the opportunity to "read" (or pretend read) about the topic. Learning centers that are literacy-enhanced:

- provide opportunities for children to develop oral language.

- encourage print awareness.

- encourage children to further explore the relationship between reading and writing.

- help children develop a natural connection between reading and writing at school and reading and writing in their world.

Determine why you want learning centers as a part of your curriculum. Some of the reasons you may have for establishing learning centers in your classroom will support student development, others may not. Some reasons may be better supported by activities other than learning centers.

	These support student development and/or may be best achieved through learning centers.	These may not support student development and/or may be best achieved through something other than learning centers.
How will learning centers benefit the children in your class?	• Students will learn to manage themselves and materials. • Students will have opportunities to explore and experiment. • Students will be able to choose whether to work alone or to work with others of their choice.	• Students will be on task and complete assigned activities. • Students will work with specified materials to practice a skill or objective. • Students will learn to work independently.
How will learning centers benefit you, the teacher?	• You will have more opportunities to observe and assess students at work. • You will have a chance to determine and promote student interests through your interaction with them. • You will have time to create anecdotal records for each child.	• You will be free to complete paperwork or notes home to parents. • You will work with individual students on remediation activities. • You will have time to grade completed papers and projects.
What can you and students accomplish through centers that cannot be easily accomplished in any other way?	• Students will play, construct, and explore. • You will observe, support, ask questions, and listen while students are engaged in centers.	• Students will complete tasks and activities that are skill-focused and easily assessable. • You will work with small groups of students while the rest of the class is working in the centers or involved in another task.

The more you can relinquish control and give students choice, the more students will learn. Classrooms that provide choice, control, and appropriate levels of challenge appear to facilitate the development of self-regulated intentional learning in students (Turner and Paris cited in Snow, et. al., 1998).

Learning centers are a necessary part of any pre-kindergarten. These young children have not mastered the skills or "reading" and "writing" so play is how they learn when not in "big group" or "circle time." However, if you give young students of any age more choices than you are prepared to live with, centers will not be successful for you. Initially, it is better to give students fewer choices and less control until you are comfortable with students being in charge of their learning. Start slowly and work toward giving students more choices and autonomy. In kindergarten, the number and kinds of materials offered in centers need to be more limited early in the year than they are later in the year.

Think through how you would like the learning centers in your room to look. Will your learning centers be more student directed or teacher-directed? Determine where you are comfortable on the continuum in relation to:

student directed ◀——————————————————————————▶ teacher-directed

time
center choice and movement
activities and materials
alone or with others

Here are some questions to consider:

How long will children be in centers?

Learning centers usually last approximately an hour in a Building-Blocks classroom. This provides children enough time to engage in one or more open-ended activities without losing interest. Plan on students spending 20-30 minutes in each center. Researchers have observed that children need 20- to 30-minute play sessions to create elaborate scripts that lead to the intentional use of literacy in dramatic play (Christie et. al., cited in Snow et. al., 1998). If the designed activities are more narrowly defined (for example, an individual activity to be completed and assessed by the teacher) an hour may be too long. Review what and how you want children to accomplish the activities within the centers. More teacher-directed activities may require less time than more student-directed activities.

Learning centers are the primary teaching vehicle for pre-kindergarten programs. Children should be in centers for most of the day.

Four-Blocks classrooms may add a time for centers to enhance student development. In these classrooms, centers usually last 30-45 minutes and may or may not occur daily.

What choices will children have?

In a Building-Blocks classroom, teachers may design one teacher-directed activity for each center that all students must complete, with students choosing the other activities they want to complete when they are finished with the first task. These other activities are usually exploring materials, using manipulatives, or playing a game—activities they already know how to do. Again, students should have as much choice as possible and you, the teacher, should be free to interact and observe as much as possible.

In pre-kindergarten classrooms, there should be few, if any, teacher-directed activities. As mentioned before, centers are the program for pre-kindergarten programs.

Four-Blocks teachers have one or two "must do" centers with several other student selected choices.

What do children do when they have completed one center?

Students of all ages should be able to choose when they are "done" with a center and they should be able to choose, within established guidelines, what they want to do next and where they want to go next. One thing you might observe is how often children move and how engaged they become at any given center. If you observe a child engaging in only one or two centers, then you may wish to encourage them to try a new center with you or another student. If you observe a child roaming from center to center, you may want to suggest they choose an activity to begin and complete. Also, make it clear to that child that the "ticket" to leaving that space is something completed and shared with you and the "ticket" into a new space or center is "room" in that center.

What centers should I have?

Limit the number of centers you establish. As a general rule, the younger the children, the fewer the choices. Younger children may find too many choices to be overwhelming. If you have too many you will be unsuccessful keeping them fresh and interesting. You will want enough centers for two to four children to be at each space. Some centers may accommodate more than four children, but generally more than four children make the learning center crowded and noisy. The space available in your classroom will also limit what can and cannot be done and how many centers you can have. Some suggested learning centers that are teacher-directed and allow choice for students are:

1. Reading or Library (Books!)

2. Writing (including writing on the computer and coached writing)

3. Home Living/Creative Play (may include puppets)

4. Community Center (could include grocery store, doctor's office, restaurant, etc.)

5. Blocks

6. Math (with manipulative and activities)

7. Art

8. Science

9. Social Studies

10. Games and Puzzles

11. Music/Movement

12. Sensory Tables (water, sand, and rice)

13. Quiet Area

14. Other – generally related to a theme of study, a field trip, or other interests shown by children

Each center should be as interesting as possible. Use complex, open-ended materials and activities to encourage students to explore and create on their own. A snowman art activity with a sample of what the completed project should look like and pre-cut circles available as a resource is not as complex or open-ended as providing several books or posters with snowman pictures and students choosing to make their own snowman from recyclable materials, paint, crayons, markers, torn paper, cotton balls, and/or clay. On a recent television show, an artist shared how he created many different animals from recycled materials found around the house, such as paintbrushes, plastic containers, sponges, etc. This would be an open-ended complex way of creating representations of animals the child has seen or studied in class in the art center.

Change materials and activities within every center once a month (for example, the first school day of the month) or change the materials and activities in a couple of centers each week. If working on a theme, the activities should change as the theme changes. For example, if you are reading *The Little Red Hen* and doing a farm unit, you would add farm books and puzzles, art activities about farm animals, farm animal puppets, farm oriented math manipulatives, etc., to each of your centers so each center has an activity related to the new theme. No matter how you teach, change or add to each center approximately every four weeks to keep them "new" and appealing.

Where do students practice words if there isn't a Words Center?

Words are integrated into the Reading and Writing Centers. The Reading Center should be a pleasant, cozy place for the students to read alone or with a friend. Teachers often use furniture that has been donated to their classroom. Some schools buy child-size chairs and sofas and other schools build a reading loft for classes to read in. There should be lots of good books and other reading materials. In the Reading Center, students will not only read books but read their classmates names, read other words posted around the room ("reading the room"), and find words on alphabet puzzles. In the Writing Center they may use sponge letters, plastic letters, and sandpaper letters to make words. The children will use also picture dictionaries to write and draw words. They may write the various words they know including names, words displayed around the room, words on charts, words from stories, rhyming words, and words of their own choice. It is important that students see words as a part of the reading and writing process, not as a separate activity of its own.

Pre-Kindergarten students will experiment with print; Four-Blocks students will use what they are learning in the Working with Words Block in their reading and writing.

Should children be expected to work alone or with others?

Students of all ages should find opportunities to do work alone and with others. If you observe children primarily working alone, you may want to encourage them to get involved in a group activity such as the Blocks Center or the Home Living Center. If you observe children rarely working alone, you may want to encourage them to go to the Art Center or the Reading Center. Young children profit from activities they do by themselves, and they also need to learn to live and work with others; centers provides children with these opportunities.

What is my role while students are working in centers?

Ideally you, the teacher, are observing, probing and scaffolding individual students, asking questions, engaging in some of the centers activities, and listening to students at work. Teachers who try to visit and interact with as many centers as possible each day find that they can "help" children when they need help without "pulling" the children to work with them one on one for interventions. When you interact with students during center time it also helps with classroom management. Some centers need adult help more than others. The Art Center, depending on the activity in that center, can often use an "extra" pair of hands if you have a teacher assistant or parent volunteer. The teacher is the one that needs to oversee and intervene in any and all centers. When you determine it is appropriate to intervene you should:

- take the child's point of view;
- consider their interests; and
- leave them room to work out their own solutions (Korat, Bahar, & Snapir, 2002).

Your interventions will be more helpful if they are conversations with your students, rather than inquisitions.

Center time is an excellent time to observe children and take anecdotal records.

You may choose to design one teacher-directed activity that all students must complete. Limit the number of these activities. You cannot be in multiple places at the same time and your direction limits student autonomy. You also want to free yourself to be an observer of student learning. Since assessment is a current trend as we write this book, appropriate assessment can be conducted and noted as teachers visit in centers.

Quality learning centers require planning and preparation. Time spent planning for centers may look different than time spent planning whole-group or individual lessons; however, the outcome, student learning, is the same. Teachers find that the time spent preparing for centers frees them to participate in centers with children. Setting up the environment so that children can learn through active involvement with each other, with adults, and with materials is a critical component of centers preparation. Consider the room arrangement, furniture needs, center management, how activities will be developed and where to find materials, how centers will be labeled and directions provided, and how teachers will keep track of student engagement and learning. Consider introducing new centers or new activities at the centers to the whole class at "big group time."

Room Arrangement

A lot of the room arrangement depends on the space you are given! You will also have to consider where your power outlets are located for a Listening Center and how close to water you are for your Water Table and painting activities. Think about how the average four-, five-, or six- year-old behaves in a large open space. To avoid roaming and running, the classroom should have small, clearly defined spaces all around the room for learning centers with large open spaces for whole-group meetings, activities, and students desks or tables. Use extra desks, tables, bookshelves, kitchen sets, dividers, cubbies, carrels, etc., to delineate each space. This provides opportunities for students to be engaged for longer periods of time, be more self-directed, and have more activity choices.

Some teachers choose to create centers that are boxed so students can take them to their seats. The benefit to this arrangement is space management. The boxes generally take up less space and can easily be repacked and stored. The drawback to centers that are boxed and taken to seats is they usually last for shorter periods of time, are more teacher-directed, and have less activity choice. You may find that the activities in a box are more suited to independent work than centers work.

All of the materials students need to be successful should be in the learning center. Pencils and paper should be at every center. If students need markers in the Art Center, Writing Center, and Block Center, a set should be provided in each space and not centrally located. Providing duplicates allows students to remain focused and limits opportunities to "roam."

Separate quiet centers from noisy centers and locate logically related centers near each other. The Reading, Writing, and Listening Centers would be well placed side by side as they are all quiet centers. The Blocks, Home Living, Puppets, Woodworking, and Music/Movement Centers would all be considered more "noisy" centers. The Science and Math Centers may be logically related if students explore concepts in the Science Center that are then counted, graphed, or used to develop patterns in the Math Center.

In Building-Blocks classrooms, we like to think that approximately 1/3 of the daily instructional time should be spent in whole-group activities, 1/3 in independent activities (that may follow up a whole-group activity), and 1/3 in learning centers. This may not be the same equation you use to determine room usage. You may determine that additional tables and desks for independent work take up too much space. Independent activities, not centers based, can be taken to desks and tables that are a part of each center. If space is limited, determine how much space is needed for whole-group instruction. Use the remaining space for centers, which can also be used during independent work.

Most pre-kindergarten classrooms have tables and desks in centers, with whole group time taking place on a large carpet. Since centers are only a small part of the Four-Blocks day, they may not be as evident. Group desks and tables near areas that will be used for centers.

Pre-Kindergarten Room Arrangement

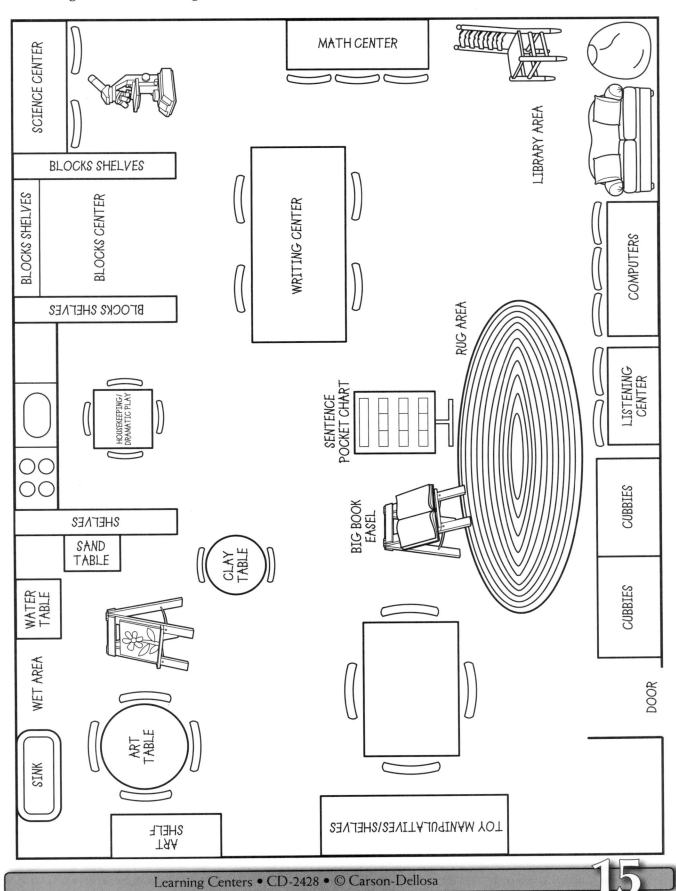

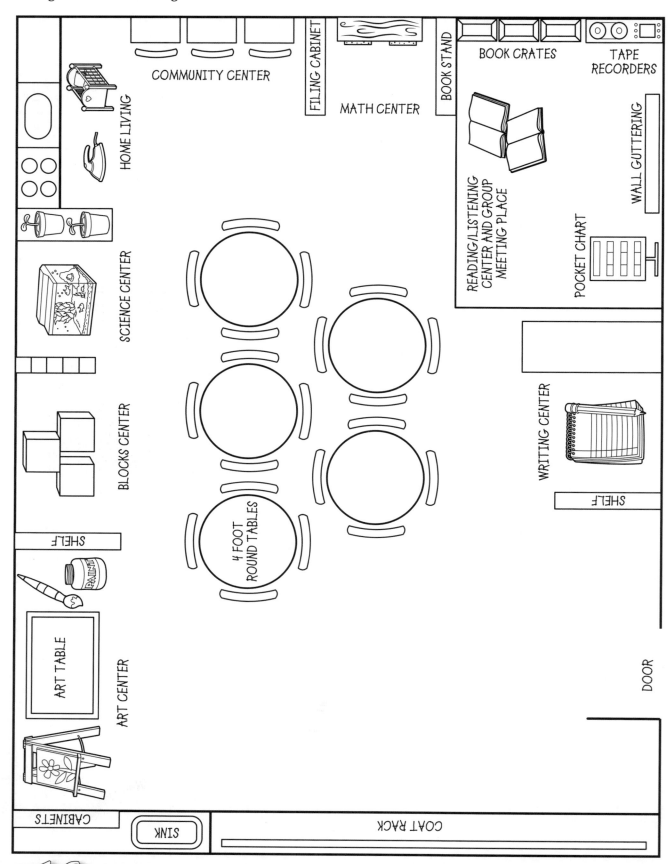

COMMUNITY CENTER

FILING CABINET

MATH CENTER

BOOK STAND

BOOK CRATES

TAPE RECORDERS

HOME LIVING

READING/LISTENING CENTER AND GROUP MEETING PLACE

WALL GUTTERING

POCKET CHART

SCIENCE CENTER

BLOCKS CENTER

WRITING CENTER

SHELF

SHELF

4 FOOT ROUND TABLES

ART TABLE

ART CENTER

DOOR

CABINETS

SINK

COAT RACK

Furniture

Besides the desks, bookshelves, kitchen set, dividers, cubbies, and carrels (those individual work spaces some children need) you will want to find other things to use to divide the room and provide storage within each center.

Each space will need a bookshelf to store the materials for the activities in that space. Since most of us don't have eight bookshelves at our disposal, consider some alternative storage units. Simple shelves can be made using boards (12"/30.5 cm wide by whatever length shelf is needed) with concrete block supports. These shelves can be painted or left natural. They will fit in low spaces such as under the chalkboard or a bulletin board.

Plastic cubes can be tied together with plastic garbage bag ties or zip ties to create a shelving unit.

If wall space is available, house guttering can be used to create a wonderful open book display in any center. Mount two or more guttering clips so that the guttering is open to the room when placed inside the clips. Guttering can easily be cut to any size. You will only need to attach the clips to the wall.

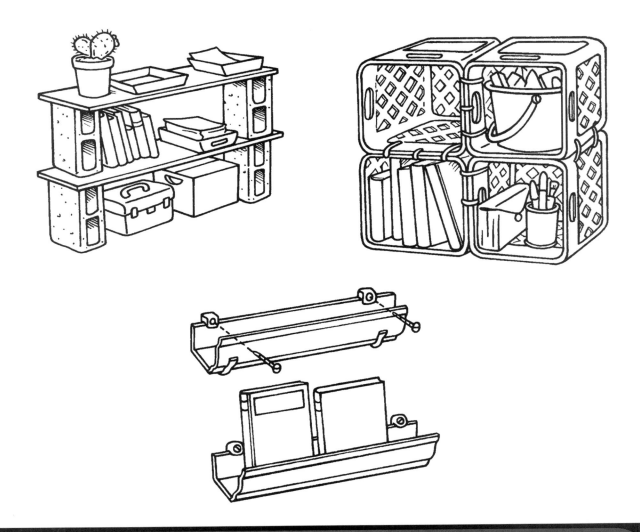

Use furniture or other barriers to divide the room into small, attractive spaces.

Don't forget garage sales and donations. Many people are willing to dispose of or donate just what you are looking for. Tell parents and other staff members what your furniture needs are. If the furniture you get needs to be painted or cleaned, allow children to help as much as possible. This makes a real-life project and they will develop a sense of ownership by helping. Have children determine what needs to be done to make the furniture usable, allow them to "order the supplies" (this is a great interactive writing activity for a Building-Blocks classroom), and let them participate in the doing. Young children love to take responsibility for their environment; it makes them feel more a part of it! Don't forget the "dollar stores" (the dime stores of today!). These are wonderful places to find inexpensive materials.

The Reading Center will need a pocket chart and chart stand. You may also choose to put a pocket chart and chart stand in the math center for graphing or the writing center in a four-year-old kindergarten so that young children can put letters or words they know together. Pocket charts can be made from poster board, laminating film, and electrical tape. Cut the poster board to the desired length and width. Cut the laminating film the same width as the poster board with each piece approximately 2"/5 cm high. Tape the laminating film in place with each piece approximately 2"/5 cm apart (4"/10 cm from bottom of one piece to bottom of next).

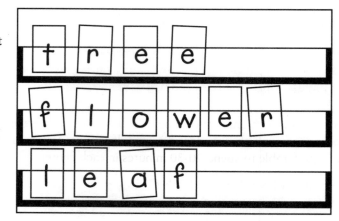

If your room does not come equipped with two or more chart stands, consider making one from rigid PVC pipe. Purchase three 10'/3 m lengths of 1" pipe, six 1" elbows, four 1" tees, and 5 shower curtain rings. Cut the 1" pipe into eight 36"/1 m lengths and four 6"/15.25 cm lengths (there will be quite a bit left over). Put the chart stand together using the elbows and tees. Attach the pocket chart with the curtain rings. The chart stand and rings can be purchased for about $10.00 (US).

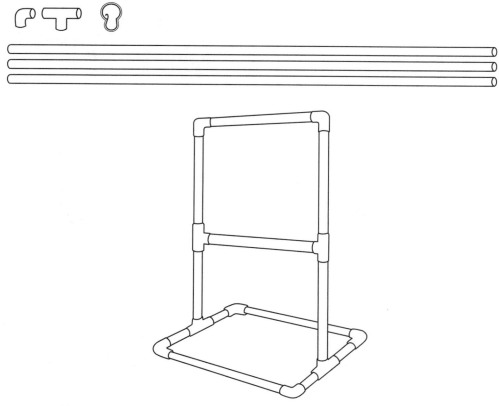

The kindergarten day runs smoothly when well planned and well managed. Activities for each center are planned by the teacher to enhance the curriculum. The learning centers should be arranged to enable children to move about easily and allow for access of materials. Management of the centers depends on planning and teacher preference.

Movement

Often teachers leave center selection to the children, guiding choices individually as needed. Other teachers schedule center activities for their students so that all students are exposed to a variety of experiences each day/week.

If students choose when to move, decide how you will help them determine when they are "done" and how they will know what their choices are. Model how you know when you have completed an exploration and how you use the planning aids in the room to choose your next center. You can use timed rotations with students staying at a center for a designated amount of time, which is teacher-directed, or students can decide when they want to move on to the next center, which is student directed. If you use timed rotations, decide how long students will spend at each center. It is preferable to spend 20-30 minutes in each center.

Number of Students at Each Center

Planning aids define how many students may be at a center at any given time. Planning aids come in many forms. The aid you choose needs to reflect how students use the centers.

If centers are more student directed, a planning aid is usually located at each center. The planning aid may be a sign, board, or can where each child hangs a name tag, a clothespin, or any other item with his name written on it. Colored dots, clothespin outlines, or hooks may designate the number of children allowable in each space. Students may move to any space that has an open dot, outline, or hook, but must wait until one opens up if all spaces are filled.

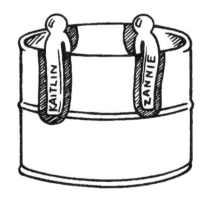

If centers are more teacher-directed, the planning aid will most likely be centrally located. These aids may be pocket charts, planning boards, or planning wheels. This type of planning aid is usually used when teachers determine which centers children will attend and how long they will stay there. Pocket charts and planning boards may resemble a graph with the names of each learning center on one side and student name cards placed by the center each child is expected to attend. Moving student names or the names of the centers makes each rotation complete. Planning wheels are similar to charts and boards. They may have student names on the outside wheel with the name of the center on the inside wheel. The wheel is rotated to show where students move next.

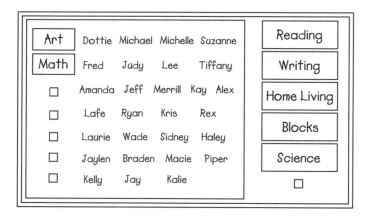
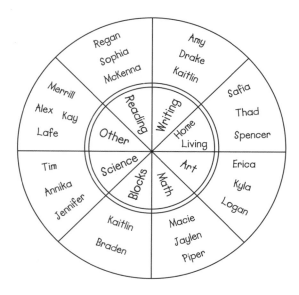

Pocket charts can be used by children to show their center choice. The pocket chart should be at students' height and should hold the center names. Each student would place her name card under or beside her choice. This would be a centrally located planning aid that allows for student choice.

Reading	Writing	Home Living	Blocks	Art	Math	Science
Kaitlin	Karen	Chris	Keith	Jurhee	Matt	Loretta
Kyla	Erica	Logan	Aaron	Amy	Sherry	Angie
Linda	Howard	Chad	Barb	Harold	Pat	Jay
Sophia	Julie	Sid	Imi	Larry	Regan	Jim

Review local and state curriculums to identify what students are expected to experience and learn in pre-kindergarten, kindergarten, or first grade. (If you do not have a local curriculum or do not like what is in the curriculum guide for your school, then get on the committee the next time the curriculum is written or revised and help to write it or change it.) When determining which activities to develop in your classroom, think about how:

- children can practice and apply the skills and concepts that have been introduced to them.
- you can promote individual work, as well as activities for small groups to work and play cooperatively.
- you can use concrete, real, and relevant learning materials.

Activities may be developed for month-by-month concepts or by themes. Examples of both are provided in this book. Each center will require a particular set of materials that are standard, or always available, as well as some materials that will be exchanged depending upon the activities. This will provide some support, as well as keep the centers fresh and engaging.

Materials for centers can be found in many places. Some teachers post teacher wish lists in the hall outside their doors. Parents and/or other teachers may fill the wish list with items they already have. Teachers may also send out a broadcast E-mail requesting particular items they need. Discount shops will have many items needed for a dollar or less. And again, don't forget garage sales. You may pick up something at little or no expense, depending on what you are looking for.

Labels and Directions

Children need to know where centers are located and what they can and should do within those spaces. They also need to know how many children are allowed in the centers. Create all of that printed information with children. This is another interactive writing activity that shows children a real purpose for reading and writing

Determine what you will call each center. Choose names that make sense to children. It may make more sense to children to call it the Math Center rather than the Manipulatives Center. Make a sign for the space that all children and adults can see. Many teachers choose to hang these from the ceilings of their classrooms. Once centers are labeled, materials will also need to be labeled. Again, think about what children would call these things. You may call them "manipulatives," but most children will call them counters or cubes. In the Art Center, label the markers, crayons, different types of paper, stamps, etc. You may also want to put a picture on the label beside the words to show what is in this container or on this shelf. By doing this activity **with** children, they will already know what each item is, as well as what the sign says about it.

It is not necessary to call attention to print in pre-kindergarten classrooms, but it is necessary to have lots of print in the room. Label the centers and objects in the room so children can learn what "words" are. Have a print-friendly environment in which a few chairs are labeled "chair" (hand written on sentence strips), the computer is labeled "computer," the printer is labeled "printer," etc. The centers are labeled with their names and a picture of what happens in that center. For example, under the label "Blocks Center" draw a few blocks and maybe the blocks put together to form an object. At the Puppet Center, have a picture of puppets on the sign. In most classrooms, it helps to draw a stick figure of how many children are allowed in each center. The cubbies are labeled with the children's names; and kindergarten children of any age can usually locate their cubbies and recognize their names. The teacher models writing every day and writes for children every day during Circle Time as she asks the usual questions (What day is it? What is the weather today?) and then writes a greeting on the board or on a piece of chart paper.

It is helpful to let students see you write and call attention to print in Building-Blocks™ classrooms. Five-year-old classrooms should also be print rich environments. Many teachers label the objects in their rooms and then label their centers by writing the names on sentence strips and putting the labels in visible places. If you are making a sign for a learning center in a Building-Blocks classroom, consider writing that sign in "big group" and not just putting it in the center. In this way, your children can see you writing (writing for children) and can hear you talking about what you are writing and why you are writing it ("a think aloud"). Some children will use the opportunity to gain print experience (left to right, top to bottom, etc.), while other children are learning letter names (as you say the letter names you are writing) or learning to read some familiar words (those high frequency words that keep popping up in all of our reading and writing). Tell the children how many students are allowed in each center and write that numeral on the sign. You may want to add five "hooks" for children's names—no more "hooks" available for name tags means no more children allowed into the center.

Write directions with children for the specific activities children can do while in each center. If children can choose to make a phone book at the Writing Center, discuss with them what they will need to do to complete the activity. If children can choose to listen to a story on tape, write the directions for using the tape recorder. Write step-by-step directions and include as many picture cues as possible.

Your interaction with students is more important than your assessment of them, however now is the time for anecdotal records if you want to keep them or if your school district requires them.

What to Track

There are many things you can track in centers. You can keep records of the center choices students make, the number of times they visit given centers, the number of activities they complete (or don't complete) within the centers, how they interact with the other students in the centers, how they use the materials within the spaces, or how engaged they become (sustained over time) in activities. However, since the goal is to track students' progress, then we would suggest that you identify any district objectives you can assess while students are working. What are you supposed to teach and what are the children supposed to learn by the end of the year? Did you observe them making a pattern or patterns in the Math Center? Were they counting? How high did they count? Did students accurately use letters and sounds to write simple messages? Any indicators of cognitive development are valuable pieces of information to record, as are improvements in social development, self-regulation, and curiosity.

How to Keep Track of Student Engagement and Learning

You may want to keep anecdotal records for each child. Many teachers find clipboards with self-stick notes or address labels a convenient way to note individual behaviors. These can then be placed in a notebook that has each child's name written on one or more pages or on individual index cards filed by student name. Some teachers also write down quotes from students as evidence of their learning.

Student sheets with checklists for given behaviors or exhibited skills may be kept on the clipboard. You may choose to observe a child for 10-15 minutes while noting behaviors on a student sheet. Or, you may choose a learning center or two each time and observe all of the children in the center(s). While the self-stick notes and address labels allow teachers to note behaviors for multiple children at one time, the student sheets tend to be more focused on an individual child.

Completed activities, copies of activities, samples, or pictures of completed activities round out the evidence of student engagement and learning.

Why to Take Time to Track Student Engagement and Learning

Teacher notes and observations along with samples of completed activities provide valuable information for reporting to parents during conferences; for assessing student learning for grade cards and evaluating the curriculum; and for evaluating how well the centers you have established are meeting your needs. If students are not engaged in meaningful ways and showing evidence of learning, then you will want to rethink how your centers are structured and what students are doing in the centers.

Some teachers explain and explore a center each day at the beginning of the school year. Other kindergarten teachers begin their centers on the first day of kindergarten; especially in four-year-old kindergarten. If you decide to begin your centers the first day, then you will want to limit the amount of materials you place in each center. The rule is to have enough materials in each center to hold the children's interest but not enough to overstimulate them or to create a problem when cleaning up. If you plan to have centers on the first day, then you must also find the time on the first day to take the whole class to each learning center and show them the individual signs and procedures for your centers. Make sure you not only *show* the children the signs, but you *tell* the children the name of each center, the number of students allowed in each center, and what they can do there. You may also want to limit the number of children in each center early in the year. As children get more comfortable with your routine and classroom, then the number of centers and the number of children in each center can be increased.

If you are a Building-Blocks or Four-Blocks teacher, you might want to plan to spend a week or two introducing the centers to the children. Children need to know what to do in each center and what you expect. The time invested up front will determine how successful students will be using the centers independently. Introduce the centers to students one center at a time. Consider starting with a center that can accommodate several children like the Reading Center or the Writing Center. Teach students the procedure for the first center and then let all of the students practice. If you start with the Reading Center, discuss how to select a book, where to go to read it, and how to put it away.

Next, you might show children how to choose a stuffed animal to read to or how to use the Special Reading Place (this may be a chair, tent, or other space depending on the month or theme). When it is practice time, draw the names of a few children to choose a stuffed animal or use the special place. Let all of the other students select books to look at, then practice how to get books and put them away. On another day, show children how to use the tape recorder to listen to books on tape. When it is practice time, draw the names of a few children to listen to books on tape, others to choose an animal to read with or use the Special Reading Place, and let all of the other students select a book to look at. Continue this practice until you feel all children clearly understand how to use the Reading Center.

Then, move on to another center such as the Writing Center. Determine what children need to know about the materials, activities, and space and introduce these one at a time. When it is practice time, have some children return to the Reading Center, while other students practice at the Writing Center. As you move from center to center, the number of students engaged at each space should begin to go down and represent what you want "real" center time to look like.

Return to these procedures when introducing new materials and activities. The center changes whenever choices change. Be sure to take time to discuss and practice what the change looks like.

Pre-Kindergarten classrooms usually start the year with all centers functioning. Determine what children need to know to be successful and get started. Don't try to wait for a week or two to introduce each center.

Reintroduce centers and procedures after lengthy breaks and when students appear to have "forgotten" the plan. This will be time well invested.

Another way to begin and end each center time is with a class meeting. This may be called PoWeR Time. This is another opportunity to remind students what they should be doing during centers. PoWeR stands for:

- Plan
- Work
- Review

PoWeR Time should take five minutes before and after centers.

When students Plan, they identify which centers they will start in and what they plan to do there. If centers are student directed, this is an opportunity for children to commit to a plan and an opportunity for the teacher to provide direction to students who need to choose a new space because the one they want is already filled. For student directed centers, teachers may want to use craft sticks with the students' names written on them to randomly determine the order in which children get to choose centers each day. Or teachers may choose to call on students in a particular order with the name of the first student called rotating each day. When a student is called on, she should be prepared to share which center she plans to attend and what she intends to do there. For teacher-directed centers, Plan Time is an opportunity to review who is going where and what they are expected to accomplish in that place. Work Time occurs while students are engaged in the learning centers. Review Time allows a few children to share what they did during centers that day and provides an opportunity for the teacher to follow up on how well centers are functioning. Each child should have a time to share sometime during the week. Names may be drawn randomly or students may be assigned a day of the week to share. Review Time should not take more than 5-10 minutes, with each child sharing for only a minute or two. Students may share what they played with, whom they played with, or what they made (which can be shared as well). The teacher should plan to ask students questions to prompt deeper thinking. This is also a time to check in to see if the child followed through with the Plan he made during Plan Time and discuss why this did or did not work out. It is also a time to help the child plan ahead for tomorrow. Future thinking may be difficult for young children, but it is important to help them think in that manner.

Have a specific signal that lets all children know center time is over and it is time to clean up. Ask children, one at a time, to practice putting their books away. Discuss how children looked at books and returned them to the correct location during Review Time.

Managing Student Behavior at Learning Centers

The best management tools are clear procedures and interesting activities that are open ended. If centers are not running smoothly, first assess the procedures and activities. Even when these are in place, some children need feedback that is concrete and specific to help them learn to manage themselves. This is another reason why you need to be available at center time.

Noise Level

You might try using music to indicate appropriate noise levels for various activities at school. Select three musical pieces: one that is slow and "quiet" (for example, classical music), one that has some movement but not too much (for example, light jazz), and one that is loud and fast (for example, rock). Locate or copy only 30-60 seconds of each selection. Use these to help students understand the difference between quiet times and places with no talking (nap time, walking down the hall, listening to announcements), work times and places with some productive talking (center time, work time, lunchroom), and active times and places with loud voices (playground). Introduce centers by listening to a short selection of "light jazz" music, review center time by listening to short selections of all three pieces of music and having students indicate which song represented today's noise level. Use the music as a discussion starter and reference point when you meet with individual children that struggle with appropriate volume levels.

Occasionally, you may tape a productive center day and let students listen to how it sounds. Then, you may tape an unproductive (noisy) day and let students listen to that. At Big Group time or PoWeR time, have a conversation about the two days. Discuss why this happens and how to avoid it in the future.

Clean Up

Be sure to discuss clean up when introducing centers and allow enough time for students to put things away. When this isn't sufficient, analyze what is breaking down.

For example:

- One particular center isn't getting cleaned up. Is there too much "stuff?" Are students stopping the activity when the signal is given? Target the specific center and work one-on-one with students in that center.

- One particular group of students isn't cleaning up. Are they stopping the activity when the signal is given? Is there one student cleaning or not cleaning? Target the specific group and/or child for some one-on-one work.

- There is a general lack of concern for the materials and space. At PoWeR Time, discuss how important it is for things to be there for the next group. Ask children to talk about how it feels when they get to a center and the materials aren't there, or they can't find what they want.

Clean up may be new to some students, but this is an important life skill. Helping them learn how and why they need to clean up will be worth investing the time.

Getting Along

Children may or may not be developmentally ready to work together cooperatively to complete a collaborative activity; however they should be able to share a space and materials. If students are having trouble getting along, analyze what the issue may be.

For example:

- Children aren't getting along at one particular center. Is there enough space? Is there enough to do? Are the activities open-ended and complex? Are students clear about what they are supposed to do in the center? Target the specific center and work with them one-on-one.

- One particular group of students isn't getting along. Are they clear about what they are supposed to do? Is there a conflict between two children? Target the specific group or child and work with them one-on-one. You may need to move children in and out of groups to create working relationships.

- Several of the children are having difficulty getting along. At Big Group time or PoWeR Time, discuss how important it is for students to get along so that they can accomplish the activities you have designed for them. Ask children to talk about how it feels to have to take time from centers to solve getting along problems. Discuss how this can be avoided.

The following sections of the book provide suggestions and starting points for developing learning centers in your classroom. The first section discusses the purpose, basic activities, teacher's role, and standard materials for each center. The second section has suggestions for monthly centers. The third section has ideas for thematic centers. The final section includes resources and resource suggestions.

> If students are not engaged in meaningful ways, or are not showing evidence of learning, take time to observe and rethink how your centers are structured and what activities you are asking students to do.

Learning Centers

Reading /Library Center (Books!)

Children develop a love for reading through many happy experiences with people and books. They need to find that books give both pleasure and information. They look at books, share books with others, listen to adults read books, and listen to taped stories. This center has a "read to" and "read by" focus. The Reading Center activities focus on looking at books, listening to books, and playing with words. This learning center provides additional opportunities for children to build a desire to learn to read, to learn interesting-to-them words, and to develop print concepts.

Basic Activities
The foundations for the activities in this center are:

- Reading books and charts
  - Picture reading by looking at the pictures and making up a story
  - "Pretend Reading" by telling a familiar story
  - Reading all of the words
- Listening to taped stories
- Making taped stories
- Reading the room
- Making words

Teacher's Role
While students are in this center, the teacher should be:

- "Blessing" books by reading them to students
- Modeling ways to read
- Listening to children "read"
- Listening to taped stories with children
- Discussing stories with children

Standard Materials
The materials that should always (well, almost always!) be available in this center are:

- Books
  - Big books
  - Read alouds ("blessed" books)

- Favorite stories
- Songs in print
- Predictable books
- Class-made predictable chart books
- Reading charts
  - Predictable charts

    A predictable chart has a predictable structure (I see . . . , I like . . . , My name is . . . , etc.) that is completed by every student in the class. The sentences on the chart are used throughout the week for reading, sentence building, and book making. The completed charts and class books are wonderful additions to the Reading Center because every child in the room is familiar with the predictable pattern and has experienced success with reading the sentences during the week. For more information and ideas see *Predictable Charts: Shared Writing for Kindergarten and First Grade* by Hall and Williams (Carson-Dellosa, 2001.)

  - Interactive charts

    Interactive charts provide opportunities for children to manipulate text and interact with print as they learn to read the text. An early-in-the-year interactive chart may be based on a nursery rhyme, traditional song, counting song, familiar poem, or finger play. Later in the year, interactive charts may be based on a theme or topic of study. Choose a word or words from the poem, rhyme, or song to be manipulated. This will be a name, a rhyming word, a number word, etc. Interactive charts in the Reading Center provide ongoing opportunities for students to practice manipulating text and interacting with print. For more information and ideas, see *Interactive Charts: Shared Reading for Kindergarten and First Grade* by Hall and Williams (Carson-Dellosa, 2001).

- Wall Charts
- Student names
- Color words
- Theme words
- Nursery rhymes on chart paper
- Cassette tape recorder with headphones
- Portable cassette tape players with headphones
- Cassette tapes (blank and pre-recorded)
- Alphabet puzzles
- Magnetic letters
- Sandpaper letters
- Sponge letters
- Overhead projector
- Book storage (shelves, guttering, tubs)
- Pocket chart and pocket chart stand
- Book stand for big books
- Carpet, beanbags, pillows

Pre-Kindergarten

The Reading Center is appropriate and necessary for pre-kindergarten. The making words manipulatives (magnetic letters, sandpaper letters, and sponge letters) may be located in a writing center. There may be some class-made books, but the books made from predictable charts and interactive charts are more suitable for five-year-old kindergarten (Building Blocks).

Four Blocks

The Reading Center is appropriate for a Four-Blocks classroom.

Mark standard materials with a colored dot. These things will stay in the center. Anything that does not have a dot should change each month.

Children live in a world with lots of print. Experiencing and experimenting with function and forms of written language are important as children grow in the ways they perceive writing. Given the opportunities and the materials, children will produce labels, lists, cards, letters, stories, and books. These early efforts at writing provide the teacher with a clear picture of the child's understanding of print. This center has a "writing by children" focus. The Writing Center activities focus on writing for real reasons, book making, and playing with words. This learning center provides additional opportunities for children to build a desire to learn to write and to learn letters and sounds.

Basic Activities

The foundations for the activities in this center are:

- Writing
  - Pictures ("telling" stories with pictures)
  - "Driting" (some drawing/some writing)
  - Writing
- Book making
- Poster making
- Class newspaper
- Interviews
- Note writing
- Making words
  - Names
  - Words found around the room
  - Words from charts
  - Words from stories
  - Rhyming words
  - Student's choice

Teacher's Role

While students are in this center the teacher should be:

- Discussing writing with children
- Encouraging children to expand on their writing
- Encouraging the use of reference materials posted around the room
- Encouraging children to refer to the "blessed" books in the Writing Center

Standard Materials

The materials that should always (well, almost always!) be available in this center are:

- Books about writing
- Books that contain good stories
- Work space (tables, desks)
- Paper (newsprint, lined, unlined, stationery)
- Blank books – half sheet of paper with construction paper cover (see pages 136-146 for shape book patterns)
- Pencils
- Magnetic board, cookie sheets, or side of file cabinet
- Magnetic letters
- Sponge letters
- Letter stamps
- Stapler, glue, tape
- Picture dictionaries
- Computer and printer

Pre-Kindergarten

The Writing Center is appropriate and necessary for a four-year-old kindergarten. However, the book making, class newspaper, and letter writing would not be a part of four-year-old kindergarten. The opportunity for pretend writing should play a bigger part of this important literacy center for four-year-olds. Children who have *not* had lots of paper, pencils, pens, and colored markers in their homes need an opportunity to experiment with writing and writing materials at school.

Four Blocks

The Writing Center is appropriate for a Four-Blocks classroom. Making books, writing letters, making a newspaper, and writing for "real" reasons are important writing activities in Four-Blocks classrooms.

Because family and home are the biggest parts of the child's world, young children like to spend time imitating the things seen and done there. Children enjoy becoming the people they know: doing their work, expressing their feelings, and using their language. This center has a language development focus. The Home Living Center activities focus on dramatic play with concrete and relevant materials. This learning center provides children with additional opportunities to build a desire to learn to read and write, develop language concepts, and develop oral and meaning vocabulary.

Basic Activities

The foundation for the activities in this center is dramatic play. Dramatic play enhances cognitive development, memory, social competence, and language skills and has positive effects on problem solving and concept development (NREL, 1998).

Teacher's Role

While students are in this center the teacher should be:

- Talking to students about their dramatizations

- Asking questions that encourage students to incorporate additional children and props

- Asking questions that encourage students to identify and solve problems that they do not yet recognize on their own

- Encouraging the use of books and writing in play

Standard Materials

The materials that should always (well, almost always!) be available in this center are:

- Furniture
- Appliances
- Dolls
- Telephone
- Dress-up clothes

- Children's magazines (*Lady Bug, Humpty Dumpty's Magazine, Your Big Back Yard, Preschool Playroom, Nick Jr., U.S. Kids*, etc.)

- Adult "home living" magazines

- Newspapers and newspaper ads

- Catalogs

- Blank paper for:

  - Grocery lists
  - Message pads (by phone)
  - Recipe cards
  - Phone book
  - Cook books

Pre-Kindergarten

The Home Living Center is appropriate and necessary for a pre-kindergarten. Young children love to pretend they are grown-ups and can do the things grown-ups do.

Four Blocks

There is usually not space for this center, nor is it needed in Four-Blocks classrooms.

When students go to the library, encourage them to find books for each center. Check out any books that students recommend or keep a list as a reminder to get these books when it is time to update the centers.

This center builds and reinforces spatial and motor skills. The Blocks Center activities focus on building, replicating, and representing real world structures, dramatic play with structures, and patterning. The Blocks Center is as popular as the Home Living Center and encourages much imagination. Building with blocks gives children a chance to think, plan, and solve problems while moving freely and working with the whole body. Building with blocks also helps children begin to conceptualize size, shape, and balance. For block play to work well, children must have space to build. This learning center provides children with additional opportunities to develop language concepts and the ability to represent objects through print.

Basic Activities
The foundations for the activities in this center are:

- Creating patterns
- Representing structures
- Representing animals

Teacher's Role
While students are in this center, the teacher should be:

- Talking to students about their projects
- Asking questions that encourage students to incorporate additional materials
- Asking questions that encourage students to identify and solve problems that children do not yet recognize on their own
- Encouraging the use of paper and pencil in representing what they have built

Standard Materials
The materials that should always (well, almost always!) be available in this center are:

- Books
- Wooden blocks of various sizes and shapes
- Shelves with patterns of block shapes on shelves (use contact paper or stencil the patterns on with paint) or a storage unit for blocks
- Sets of farm animals and/or zoo animals (any type or material)
- Small cars, trains, etc. (any type or material)
- Sets of community people (any type or material)
- Sets of landscape pieces (any type or material)
- Boxes, boards, barrels, spools
- Milk cartons or other containers
- Blank paper for representation
- Graph paper for representation
- Pencils and crayons for drawing representations

Pre-Kindergarten
The Blocks Center is appropriate and necessary for a pre-kindergarten. The building and replicating of objects is more important than the drawing of them at this stage of development.

Four Blocks
There is usually not space for this center, nor is it needed in a Four-Blocks classroom.

The more children know and understand about their world, the more independent and confident they become. The child is always encouraged to ask questions, look for answers, and become aware of what is going on around her. Using magnets, caring for pets, and growing plants are just a few ways to give children new experiences to think about and new things to try out. This center focuses on observation and play. Collections of rocks, leaves, or magnets may be displayed for children. The Science Center activities revolve around looking at plants, animals, and simple machines. In this center, you will find science books, as well as ideas for experiments and materials for recording observations. This learning center provides additional opportunities for children to build a desire to learn to read and write, learn "interesting to them" words, and develop language concepts, as well as oral and meaning vocabularies.

Basic Activities

The foundations for the activities in this center are:

- Observing and caring for plants
- Observing, writing directions for care, and caring for live animals

  (Unlike other center materials, when new animals are added they should remain in the center for the rest of the school year.)
- Using and observing other science materials (magnets, simple machines, etc.) during the year
- Performing experiments, including reading and writing in response to experiments

Teacher's Role

While students are in this center the teacher should be:

- Asking questions about observations
- Encouraging children to record observations
- Encouraging children to use books found in the center

Standard Materials

The materials that should always (well, almost always!) be available in this center are:

- Theme-based books
- Large and small magnifying glasses
- Materials for recording (paper, pencils, etc.)
- Timer for animal observations
- Materials needed for the simple science experiments (examples: magnets, seeds, soil, water, scales, etc.)
- Small mirrors
- Flashlights
- Gardening tools

- Magnets (bar, cylindrical, horseshoe)
- 10-20 gallon aquarium or terrarium
- Simple machines (such as pulleys)
- Animals (frogs, turtles, grasshoppers, guinea pigs, beetles, crickets, caterpillar/butterfly, and other creatures from the everyday world.)

Sometimes these materials will *not* show up until the class is studying a theme or topic. They remain there for the rest of the year or as long as the children are using them.

Pre-Kindergarten

The Science Center is appropriate for a pre-kindergarten. A theme or unit of study may provide certain activities for this center. Experimenting, observing, and discussing are often more important than recording or written responses at this age.

Four Blocks

Exploring Science topics and hands-on experiences are important in Four-Blocks classrooms. Reading and writing related to science topics and experiments are also important; a Science Center can be a place for these extensions.

Interesting materials for sorting, comparing, and measuring are found here. This center focuses on counting, recording, and play. The Math Center activities revolve around developing patterns, measuring, counting, and finding math concepts in books. This learning center provides additional opportunities for children to build a desire to learn to read and write, to learn "interesting to them" words, and to develop language concepts and oral and meaning vocabulary.

Basic Activities

The foundations for the activities in this center are:

- Patterning
- Sorting/Classifying
- Weighing
- Data collection and graphing
- Measuring
- Estimating

Teacher's Role

While students are in this center the teacher should be:

- Encouraging the development of more complex patterns
- Asking questions about sorting and classifying
- Encouraging children to record data collection and develop graphs
- Discussing measurements with children
- Discussing estimates with children
- Encouraging children to use books as reference

Standard Materials

The materials that should always (well, almost always!) be available in this center are:

- Books
- Marker boards
- Links, gaming chips, counters
- Colored wooden or plastic beads and string
- Buttons, beads, beans, bottle tops, washers, shells, rocks, craft sticks, etc.
- Pattern blocks
- Unifix® cubes or similar cubes
- Simple balance scale and a set of weights (for example, teddy bear weights, gram weights, etc.)
- Domestic scales

- Measuring utensils (cups, jugs, spoons, containers, etc.)
- Real clock and a play clocks with moveable hands
- Egg timer
- Dominoes, dice, playing cards
- Abacus, counting frames
- Number and shape puzzles
- Real and play money (bills and coins)
- Sensory table
- Games and puzzles

Pre-Kindergarten

A Math Center with a variety of math manipulatives to compare, count, and play with is important and appropriate for a pre-kindergarten.

Four Blocks

A variety of math manipulatives are used in Four-Blocks classrooms at math time for hands-on, minds-on experiences. Reading and writing related to math topics and experiments are also important, and a Math Center can be a natural extension of these activities.

Art activities, particularly easel painting, are popular activities in kindergarten. Through a variety of different media, children are able to express ideas and feeling. In time, fine motor skills and hand/eye coordination develop. This center focuses on observation, recording, and creativity. The Art Center activities revolve around representing things in the child's world. The Art Center provides children with additional opportunities to build language concepts and represent objects through a variety of media.

Visual representations are not just decorative products to be taken home at the end of the day. They should serve as resources for further exploration and deepening knowledge of a given topic. Educators in Reggio Emilia, an Italian city with a unique collection of schools for young children, refer to visual representations as graphic languages. They speak of children "reading" their own and each other's drawings (Edwards, 1993).

Basic Activities
The foundation for the activities in this center are:

- Creating objects with recyclable materials and writing directions
- Painting and/or drawing and labeling pictures
- Making clay structures
- Developing murals

Teacher's Role
While students are in this center the teacher should be:

- Asking questions about projects
- Encouraging the use of more or different materials
- Encouraging the use of books as models and sources of information

Standard Materials
The materials that should always (well, almost always!) be available in this center are:

- Art/drawing books
- Double-sided easel
- Hanging/drying rack
- Access to water (sink or tub)
- Scraps
  - Paper
  - Fabric
- Wallpaper books
- Beautiful junk
- Markers, crayons, pencils
- Brushes, tempera paint
- Paper
- Sponges

- Yarn
- Scissors, tape, paste, glue or glue sticks
- Recyclables
  - Toilet paper tubes
  - Buttons
  - Ribbon
  - Anything that can be used to create art
- Clay/fun dough
- Pie crimper
- Garlic press
- Plastic mats for working

Some materials are not placed in the center until the children have been taught how to use them.

Pre-Kindergarten
An Art Center with a variety of art materials is important and appropriate for a pre-kindergarten. This is a center that may need an extra pair of hands (teacher assistant or parent volunteer) and some materials will not be placed in the center until the children have been taught how to use them.

Four Blocks
The Art Center is useful in a Four-Blocks classroom. Some children can express themselves better through pictures than through writing. Creating puppets and costumes for plays and "doing the book" in response to reading is important in Four-Blocks classrooms. The Art Center is a great place for children to have this opportunity.

These centers provide opportunities to further explore specific topics or ideas children are interested in pursuing. These may result from explorations in one of the established centers, a topic of study, a field trip, or any other spark.

Ideas for other centers include:

Woodworking or Construction Center

In the Construction Center, students make things using tools such as hammers, screwdrivers, etc. The objects they construct should have a use that would be helpful to others. Students would write about their construction and try to convince others that it is useful.

Sensory Center

This is a center where children explore with water, sand, salt, rice, etc. A Sensory Center is useful when children need tactile practice with letters and words. Water and sand can also be part of a Science Center and as part of a Writing Center if space is limited. A sensory table can also be used in the math center.

Zoo Center

The Zoo Center could be a follow-up to a field trip or a topic of study. In this center, students would make, read about, create patterns with, count, and continue to study zoo animals.

Gorilla (or any other animal being studied) Center

The Gorilla (or other specific animal) Center could be a follow-up to a field trip or a topic of study. In this center, students would make, read about, write about, count, and continue to learn about gorillas (or other specific animals).

Music and Movement Center

In the Music and Movement Center, young children learn to use instruments and make music. Students may listen to songs, read music and write their own music. They can also learn how to respond to musical instruments through movement. Music and movement can also be used for opposites, positional words, describing words, and visualizing as a comprehension strategy.

Puzzles and Games

This center should focus on learning how to play simple card and board games, as well as exploring simple to complex puzzles.

Add any other center you can think of and have space for!

Read aloud books that are related to a center's monthly or theme activities. These "blessed" books can then be placed in the centers.

August/September

Month-by-Month Materials & Activities

Reading · Writing · Home Living · Community · Blocks · Science · Math · Art

READING CENTER

New Materials:

• **Books**

Alphabet Books

A Book of Letters by Ken Wilson-Max (Cartwheel Books, 2002)

Chicka Chicka Boom Boom by John Archambault (Aladdin Library, 2000)

Rhyming Books

The Little School Bus by Carol Roth (North South Books, 2002)

Oh, the Places You'll Go! by Dr. Seuss (Random House, 1990)

When Dinosaurs Go to School by Linda Martin (Chronicle Books, 2002)

Back-to-School Books

First Day Jitters by Julie Danneberg (Charlesbridge Publishing, 2000)

First Day, Hooray! by Nancy Poydar (Holiday House, 2000)

Froggy Goes to School by Jonathan London (Puffin Books, 1998)

I Started School Today by Karen G. Frandsen (Children's Book Press, 1994)

If You Take a Mouse to School by Laura Numeroff (Laura Geringer Books, 2002)

Look Out Kindergarten Here I Come! by Nancy Carlson (Puffin Books, 1999)

Miss Bindergarten Gets Ready for Kindergarten by Joseph Slate (Puffin Books, 2001)

Will I Have a Friend? by Miriam Cohen (Aladdin Library, 1989)

• **Props from the Class Activity "Doing the Book"**

See *Month-by-Month Reading, Writing, and Phonics for Kindergarten* by Hall and Cunningham (Carson-Dellosa, 1997, 2003).

• **Purchased Tapes/CDs**

Chicka Chicka Boom Boom by John Archambault (Simon & Schuster, 1991)

Arthur Writes a Story by Marc Brown (Little Brown Audio, 1999)

• **Sentence Strips for Interactive Chart**

"Getting to Know You" (See page 27 for more on interactive charts.)

• **Star Wand for Reading the Room**

Star shape attached to the end of a pointer or yard stick

• **Teddy Bears for Reading Buddies**

• **Child's Lawn Chair for the Special Reading Place**

Place a child's lawn chair in a corner of the center for the Special Reading Place.

Suggested Activities with New and Existing Materials:

Students can…

• read the new books in the center to themselves or to the reading buddies.

• listen to the new stories on tape.

• complete and read other students' "Getting to Know You" charts.

• read the room with the wand. This activity can be done individually or in pairs.

• read in the Special Reading Place.

WRITING CENTER

New Materials:

- **Books**

    I Started School Today by Karen G. Frandsen (Children's Book Press, 1994)

    Arthur Writes a Story by Marc Brown (Little, Brown and Company, 1996)

- **August/September Picture Dictionary Chart from *Building-Blocks "Plus" for Kindergarten Bulletin Board* Set (Carson-Dellosa, 1998)**

    This is a chart with familiar August/September pictures and school words.

Suggested Activities with New and Existing Materials

Students can...

- make an August/September picture dictionary by stapling 5-10 pieces of paper inside colored construction paper covers, then copying a word and drawing a picture on each page.

- develop a class book with the pictures and names of each student in class. The name wall in the center, as well as the daily Getting To Know You activities will support students.

- retell a story you have read aloud previously or a story they already know.

- write notes to friends in class. Determine how you want the notes to be delivered so they do not interrupt other learning center activities.

HOME LIVING CENTER

New Materials:

- **Back-to-School Magazines, Catalogs, Newspaper Ads**
- **"Teacher" Clothes**
- **"New" Children's Clothes**

    Leave in a shopping bag for students to unpack.

Suggested Activities with New and Existing Materials:

Students can...

- make lists of the back to school items they need.

- pretend to be students going to school or parents sending their children to school.

> Separate quiet centers from noisy centers and locate logically related centers near each other.

COMMUNITY CENTER

Hair Salon

New Materials:

- **Wigs**
- **Foam Head/Wig Stand**
- **Comb**
- **Brush**
- **Curlers**

- **Barrettes and Hair Clips**
- **Spray Bottle**
- **Appointment Book**
- **Telephone**
- **Message Pad**
- **Magazines with Hair Styles**

Suggested Activities with New and Existing Materials:

Students can…

- pretend to be a stylist or a receptionist at a hair salon. Styling should be done on wigs rather than each other.

- pretend to get their "children" ready for school by going to the hair salon. Stylists performing "haircuts" should not have any equipment that might touch more than one head.

- read the magazines in the salon to find a hairstyle they like.

BLOCKS CENTER

New materials:

- **No new materials**

Suggested Activities with Existing Materials:

Students can…

- spend time getting familiar with the blocks. They can build anything that interests them.

- represent their structures on graph paper or blank paper. Post representations in the center.

SCIENCE CENTER

New Materials:

- **Plants—Fruit: Apples**

  Place green, yellow, and red apples of various sizes in the center.

- **Balance Scale and Weights**

  For example, teddy bear weights, gram weights, etc.

- **Animals—Fish**

  The fish will need an aquarium or bowl, rocks, and appropriate food. Some fish will require oxygenation systems.

  A Beta makes a good classroom fish. Betas don't require an oxygenation system and they can live in very small containers. Goldfish may not be the best fish to purchase. They do require oxygenation. Once added, the fish should remain in the center for the rest of the school year.

Suggested Activities with New and Existing Materials:

Students can…

- weigh the apples and then sort them by weight, color, and size.

- observe the fish. They should note if the fish has a particular place in the bowl that it likes to be. They should use the magnifying glass to see if they can identify any specific details. Details should be recorded in a drawing of the fish.

- write and post directions for taking care of the fish.

New Materials:

- **Books**

  Fish Eyes by Lois Ehlert (Voyager Books, 1992)

  One Little Mouse by Dori Chaconas (Viking Children's Books, 2002)

- **August/September Pattern Cards (page 147)**

- **Apples of Various Sizes and Colors**

Suggested Activities with New and Existing Materials:

Students can…

- use gaming chips to make simple patterns found on the August/September pattern cards.

- sort the apples by color and size.

ART CENTER

New Materials:

- **Books**

  Ed Emberley's Drawing Book of Faces by Ed Emberley (Little, Brown and Company, 1992)

  Looking at Faces in Art by Joy Richardson (Gareth Stevens, 2000)

  When the Root Children Wake Up by Audrey Wood (Scholastic, Inc., 2002)

- **Apples from the Science and Math Centers**

  When they need to be replaced

- **Cutting Tools**

  Plastic knives, plastic spoons, and toothpicks for carving apples

- **Mirrors**

Suggested Activities with New and Existing Materials:

Students can…

- construct a self-portrait from the recyclable materials.

- paint and/or draw a self-portrait.

- carve apples to look like themselves. Leave the apple in the center to dry.

Children need opportunities to learn to manage themselves. They also need opportunities to learn to manage materials.

READING CENTER

New Materials:

- **Books**

  Alphabet Books

  The Alphabet Tree by Leo Lionni (Knopf, 1990)

  My Beastie Book of ABC by David Frampton (HarperCollins, 2002)

  Rhyming Books

  Green Eggs and Ham by Dr. Seuss (Random House, 1960)

  Sheep in a Jeep by Nancy Shaw (Houghton Mifflin, 1997)

  Toes Have Wiggles, Kids Have Giggles by Harriet Ziefert (Putnam Publishing Group, 2002)

  Halloween Books

  Big Pumpkin by Erica Silverman (Aladdin Library, 1995)

  Five Little Pumpkins by Iris Van Rynbach (Boyds Mills Press, 2003)

  The Hallo-Wiener by Dav Pilkey (Scholastic, Inc., 1995)

  Halloween by Miriam Nerlove (Albert Whitman & Company, 1989)

  It's Pumpkin Time by Zoe Hall (Scholastic, Inc., 1999)

- **Props from the Class Activity "Doing the Book"**

  See *Month-by-Month Reading, Writing, and Phonics for Kindergarten* by Hall and Cunningham (Carson-Dellosa, 1997, 2003).

- **Purchased Tapes/CDs**

  Green Eggs and Ham by Dr. Seuss (Random House, 1987)

- **Teacher-Made Tapes**

  It's Pumpkin Time by Zoe Hall (Scholastic, Inc., 1999)

- **Sentence Strips for Interactive Charts**

  "Getting to Know You" (remainder of class), "Jack Be Nimble," "Rain" (See page 27 for more information on interactive charts.)

- **Predictable Chart**

  "Things I Like" (See page 27 for more information on predictable charts.)

  - Chart of sentences
  - Cards for sentence building
  - Class book

- **Fly Swatter for Reading the Room**

  You may want to cut out an area in the middle to highlight words.

- **Stuffed Toy Storybook Characters for Reading Buddies**

  Arthur, Spot, Madeline, etc.

- **Pumpkin Patch for the Special Reading Place**

  Make the pumpkin patch by placing bean bags and pillows in a corner with "vines" around the area.

Suggested Activities with New and Existing Materials:

Students can...

- read the books in the center to themselves or to the reading buddies, with emphasis on the new books.

- listen to the stories on tape, with emphasis on the new stories.

- complete and read the interactive charts and predictable charts made during the month.

- read the room with the fly swatter. This activity can be done individually or in pairs.

- read in the Special Reading Place.

New Materials:

- **Books**

  How a Book Is Made by Aliki (HarperTrophy, 1988)

  Halloween by Miriam Nerlove (Albert Whitman & Company, 1989)

  It's Pumpkin Time by Zoe Hall (Scholastic, Inc., 1999)

- **October Picture Dictionary Chart from *Building-Blocks "Plus" for Kindergarten Bulletin Board* Set (Carson-Dellosa, 1998)**

  This is a chart with familiar October words and pictures such as Halloween, pumpkin, leaves, etc.

- **Orange Paper—Copy and Construction**

- **Blank Shape Books—Leaves and Pumpkins**

  You can make the outline of the shape or you can purchase large shaped notepads from your local school supply store. Once you determine what shape you will use, cut blank paper to match. Each book should have 4-5 blank pages.

- **Shape Stamps—Halloween Shapes**

  Candy, ghosts, and pumpkins

Suggested Activities with New and Existing Materials:

Students can...

- continue to develop a class book with the pictures and names of each student in class. The remaining students will complete their "Getting To Know You" activities this month.

- retell a story you have read aloud previously or a story they already know.

- make a Halloween alphabet book. Encourage students to write words and draw pictures for as many letters of the alphabet as they can. You may choose to put finished books in the Reading Center.

- make Halloween books. Encourage students to use words on the Picture Dictionary chart, as well as words from Halloween books. You may choose to put finished books in the Reading Center.

New Materials:

- **Halloween Magazines, Catalogs, Newspaper Ads**
- **Clothes**
- **Halloween Costumes**

Suggested Activities with New and Existing Materials:

Students can...

- make lists of what they need for trick or treating or a Halloween party.

- get "children" ready for Halloween.

Repair Shop

New Materials:

- **Old Appliances with Electrical Cords Removed**

  Curling irons, toasters, tape recorders, etc.

- **Screwdrivers**
- **Pliers**
- **Muffin Tins**
- **Aprons or Denim Shirts**

Suggested Activities with New and Existing Materials:

Students can...

- work in the repair shop. Students can take apart appliances and sort the parts (screws, springs, etc.) in the muffin tins. Sorted items will go with the recyclables in the Art Center at the end of the month.

- send or get appliances from the shop.

New Materials:

- **Books**

  Nora's Room by Jessica Harper (HarperCollins, 2001)

  Robin's Room by Margaret Wise Brown (Hyperion Press, 2002)

  Miss Nelson Is Missing! by Harry Allard (Houghton Mifflin, 1985)

- **Small Toy People**
- **Small Model Trees**

  Remove at the end of the month.

Suggested Activities with New and Existing Materials:

Students can…

- make models of their bedrooms or classroom.
- represent their structures on graph paper or blank paper. Post representations in the center.

New Materials:

- **Plants—Vegetables: Small Pumpkins or Gourds**
- **Balance Scale and Weights**

  For example, teddy bear weights, gram weights, etc.

- **Insects—Rotting Log**

  Find a good-sized rotting log. Put the log in a large plastic container (approximately 58 quart/55 liter depending upon the size of the log) with lid. Add a small amount of soil. The log should be full of insects, and hopefully larvae, for children to observe. The insects will stay in the container as long as the lid is on when not in use. The insects are decomposing (eating) the log. Students should notice that dirt is "growing" in the bottom of the container. The only care for the log is a light misting of water every day. The log should remain in the center as long as insects are found. Insects and larvae can be "hunted" and added in the spring.

  - Spray bottle
  - Plastic spoons
  - Petri dishes or any other small dishes (for example, disposable sundae dishes from an ice cream store)
  - Magnifying glasses

Suggested Activities with New and Existing Materials:

Students can…

- weigh the pumpkins.
- sort pumpkins by weight, size, and possibly shape.
- observe the insects on rotten log. Students can put a scoop of dirt in one of the dishes to see if they can find anything with the magnifying glass.
- collect bugs from the log and place them in the dishes for further observation.
- write and post directions for taking care of the insects on rotten log (only need to keep log moist).
- continue to observe and care for the fish.

New Materials:

- **Books**

  Anno's Counting Book by Mitsumasa Anno (HarperTrophy, 1986)

  Mrs. McTats and Her Houseful of Cats by Alyssa Satin Capucilli (Margaret K. McElderry Books, 2001)

- **October Pattern Cards (page 147)**

- **Variety of Halloween Shapes**

  Happy pumpkins, sad pumpkins, big pumpkins, small pumpkins, orange pumpkins, blue pumpkins, etc.

Suggested Activities with New and Existing Materials:

Students can…

- make simple patterns on the October pattern cards using beads and string.

- sort and classify Halloween shapes.

New Materials:

- **Books**

  1-2-3 Draw Pets and Farm Animals: A Step by Step Guide by Freddie Levin (Peel Productions, 2000)

  Backyard Detective: Critters Up Close by Nic Bishop (Scholastic, Inc., 2002)

  Barnyard Banter by Denise Fleming (Henry Holt and Company, Inc., 2001)

  Ed Emberley's Drawing Book of Animals by Ed Emberley (Little, Brown and Company, 1994)

  How Artists See Animals by Colleen Carroll (Abbeville Press, Inc., 1999)

  Looking at Nature by Brigitte Baumbusch (Stewart, Tabori & Chang, 1999)

Suggested Activities with New and Existing Materials:

Students can…

- make animals using the recyclable materials. (Encourage students to use the resource materials in the center as they create their animals.)

- paint and/or draw animals from the Science Center (page 42).

- paint and/or draw color wheels. (Encourage students to use resources to determine what colors to use and how to place them on the wheels.)

Don't throw anything away without considering how it might be used in the Art Center. Your trash may be used to create a treasure!

Month-by-Month Materials & Activities

| Reading | Writing | Home Living | Community | Blocks | Science | Math | Art |

READING CENTER

New Materials:

- **Books**

  Alphabet Books

  Alphabet Soup: A Feast of Letters by Scott Gustafson (The Greenwich Workshop Press, 1994)

  Maisy's ABC by Lucy Cousins (Candlewick Press, 1995)

  What Pete Ate from A-Z by Maira Kalman (Puffin Books, 2003)

  Rhyming Books

  I Wonder Why by Lois Rock (Chronicle Books, 2001)

  Jamberry by Bruce Degen (HarperTrophy, 1985)

  November/Thanksgiving Books

  Autumn: An Alphabet Acrostic by Steven Schnur (Clarion Books, 1997)

  Cranberry Thanksgiving by Wende and Harry Devlin (Scott Foresman, 1990)

  I Know an Old Lady Who Swallowed a Pie by Alison Jackson (Puffin Books, 2002)

  In November by Cynthia Rylant (Harcourt, 2000)

  One Tough Turkey by Steven Kroll (Holiday House, 1982)

  Today Is Thanksgiving! by P. K. Hallinan (Ideals Children Books, 2001)

  'Twas the Night Before Thanksgiving by Dav Pilkey (Orchard Books, 1990)

- **Props from the Class Activity "Doing the Book"**
  See *Month-by-Month Reading, Writing, and Phonics for Kindergarten* by Hall and Cunningham (Carson-Dellosa, 1997, 2003).

- **Purchased Tapes/CDs**
  Jamberry by Bruce Degen (HarperFestival, 1998)

- **Teacher-Made Tapes**
  In November by Cynthia Rylant (Harcourt, 2000)

  Today Is Thanksgiving by P. K. Hallinan (Ideals Children Books, 2001)

- **Sentence Strips for Interactive Charts**
  "Cookie Jar," "Polly and Sukey," "A My Name is . . ." (See page 27 for more information on interactive charts.)

- **Predictable Chart**
  "I Am Thankful For..." (See page 27 for more information on predictable charts.)
  - Chart with sentences
  - Cards for sentence building
  - Class book

- **Finger Wand for Reading the Room**
  A hand shape or glove with index finger sticking out attached to the end of a pointer or yard stick

- **Thanksgiving Stuffed Toys for Reading Buddies**
  Turkey, fruits, vegetables, etc.

- **Mural for the Special Reading Place**
  Hang a large sheet of paper for a mural in the Reading Center. Have students place completed fall artwork from Art Center on the paper to create the mural.

Suggested Activities with New and Existing Materials:

Students can…

- read the books in the Reading Center to themselves or to the reading buddies, with emphasis on the new books.

- listen to the stories on tape, with emphasis on the new stories.

- complete and read the interactive charts and predictable charts made during the month.

- read the room with the finger wand. This activity can be done individually or in pairs.

- read in the Special Reading Place.

WRITING CENTER

New Materials:

- **Books**

    One Tough Turkey by Steven Kroll (Holiday House, 1982)

    Autumn: An Alphabet Acrostic by Steven Schnur (Clarion Books, 1997)

    What Do Authors Do? by Eileen Christelow (Houghton Mifflin, 1997)

- **November Picture Dictionary Chart from *Building-Blocks "Plus" for Kindergarten Bulletin Board* Set (Carson-Dellosa, 1998)**

    This is a chart with familiar November words and pictures such as turkey, Thanksgiving, family, pilgrims, etc.

- **Tan Paper—Copy and Construction**

- **Blank Shape Books—Cornucopia and Turkey**

    You can make the outline of the shape or you can purchase large shaped notepads from your local school supply store. Once you determine what shape you will use, cut blank paper to match. Each book should have 4-5 blank pages.

- **Shape Stamps—Thanksgiving Shapes**

    Turkey, pilgrims, and food

Suggested Activities with New and Existing Materials:

Students can…

- retell a story you have read aloud previously or a story they already know.

- make a Thanksgiving alphabet book. Encourage students to write words and draw pictures for as many letters of the alphabet as they can. You may choose to put finished books in the Reading Center.

- make Thanksgiving books. Encourage students to use words on the Picture Dictionary chart, as well as words from Thanksgiving books. You may choose to put finished books in the Reading Center.

- make a book from the predictable chart posted in the Reading Center.

HOME LIVING CENTER

New Materials:

- **Fall Magazines, Catalogs, Newspaper Ads**
- **Fall Clothes**
- **Cardboard Boxes**

    About the size of a copy paper box

Suggested Activities with New and Existing Materials:

Students can…

- sort and change play clothes from summer to fall. Summer clothes should be boxed, labeled, and put away until May.

- plan and take a fall vacation.

Transportation

New Materials:

• **Books**

Airport by Byron Barton (HarperTrophy, 1987)

All Aboard ABC by Doug Magee and Robert Newman (Cobblehill, 1990)

The Big Red Bus by Judy Hindley (Candlewick Press, 2000)

Car Wash by Sandra Steen and Susan Steen (Puffin Books, 2003)

Cars by Anne Rockwell (Puffin Books, 1992)

Freight Train by Donald Crews (HarperTrophy, 1992)

I Love Trains! by Philemon Sturges (HarperTrophy, 2003)

Lisa's Airplane Trip by Anne Gutman and Georg Hallensleben (Knopf, 2001)

Next Stop Grand Central by Maira Kalman (Puffin Books, 2001)

Planes by Anne Rockwell (Puffin Books, 1993)

Richard Scarry's Cars and Trucks and Things That Go by Richard Scarry (Van Nostrand Reinhold, 1974)

Round Trip by Ann Jonas (HarperTrophy, 1990)

School Buses by Dee Ready (Bridgestone Books, 1997)

Trains by Anne Rockwell (Puffin Books, 1993)

Trash Trucks by Daniel Kirk (Putnam Publishing Group, 1997)

Truck by Donald Crews (HarperTrophy, 1991)

Two Little Trains by Margaret Wise Brown (Harpercollins Juvenile Books, 2003)

The Wheels on the Bus by Paul O. Zelinsky (Dutton Books, 1990)

• **Car, Bus, Train, and/or Plane**

Create a car, bus, train, and/or plane by taping off an area in the center and placing chairs within it.

- Clothing and accessories for drivers, pilots, flight attendants, passengers
- Seat belts
- Radio
- Steering wheels
- Horns
- Tickets

Suggested Activities with New and Existing Materials:

Students can…

- elaborate on their favorite transportation. Encourage students to use the reference materials in the center to create a more "realistic" bus, train, etc.
- drive/pilot the transportation units. Students should be able to tell where they are going and how they will get there.
- ride the transportation units. Students should be able to tell where they are going and what they will do when they get there.

New Materials:

• **Books**

Froggy Goes to School by Jonathan London (Puffin Books, 1998)

Miss Bindergarten Gets Ready for Kindergarten by Joseph Slate (Puffin Books, 2001)

My Teacher Sleeps in School by Leatie Weiss (Puffin Books, 1985)

• **Small Toy People**

Remove at the end of the month.

Suggested Activities with New and Existing Materials:

Students can…

- build their school. Encourage students to refer to the books in the center for construction and extension ideas.
- represent their structures on graph paper or blank paper. Post representations in the center.

New Materials:

- **Plants—Leaves, Nuts, Seeds**
- **Light Table**

  Directions for making a light table can be found at *http://www.spec-tru.com/build_a_light_table.htm.*

- **Animals—Add a Small Mammal**

  Hamster, gerbil, mouse, etc.

  The mammal should remain in the Science Center for the rest of the school year.

- **10-20 Gallon Aquarium with Mesh Lid or Small Mammal Cage**
- **Animal Bedding**

  Pine shavings, recycled paper bedding, cedar shavings, etc.

- **Toilet Paper Tubes**
- **Food for the Mammal**
- **Toys for the Mammal**

Suggested Activities with New and Existing Materials:

Students can…

- sort and classify leaves, nuts, seed, and any other fall objects available in the center.
- take a fall walk to add to the fall objects.
- observe leaves using the light table taking particular note of the veins. Leaf observations should be carefully recorded and posted.
- observe the new animal. Students should note particular areas the animal likes and what it tends to do with most of its time.
- write and post directions for taking care of the new animal.
- continue to observe and care for the fish and the insects on the rotten log.

MATH CENTER

New Materials:

- **Books**

  One Duck Stuck by Phyllis Root (Candlewick Press, 2003)

  One Gray Mouse by Katherine Burton (Kids Can Press, 2002)

- **November Pattern Cards (pages 148-152)**
- **Variety of Snack Crackers**
- **Variety of Nuts**

Suggested Activities with New and Existing Materials:

Students can…

- make simple patterns on November pattern cards using pattern blocks.
- sort and classify snack crackers by size, shape, color, and taste.
- weigh and sort nuts by size, color, and weight.

Each learning center should provide children with opportunities to explore real reasons for reading and writing.

New Materials:

Books

A Child's Book of Art: Discover Great Paintings by Lucy Micklethwait (Dorling Kindersley Publishing, 1999)

Color by Ruth Heller (Puffin Books, 1999)

Mouse Paint by Ellen Stoll Walsh (Voyager Books, 1995)

When Autumn Comes by Robert Maass (Owlet, 1992)

Why Is Blue Dog Blue? by George Rodrigue (Stewart, Tabori & Chang, 2002)

Cornucopia (Still Life)

Suggested Activities with New and Existing Materials:

Students can…

- make fall objects seen in the Science Center (leaves, nuts, seeds, etc.) using recyclable materials and glue on the mural in the Reading Center.

- paint and/or draw a cornucopia (still life). Encourage students to label the food in their pictures.

- make fruit and vegetables from clay. Have a place for students to lay their "food" to dry. Dry pieces can be painted to look like real food.

Books that are used in the Art Center may be "picture" read without referring to the actual words on the pages. This focuses children on the pictures and allows books that may be more challenging to be usefully integrated into the center.

Month-by-Month Materials & Activities

| Reading | Writing | Home Living | Community | Blocks | Science | Math | Art |

READING CENTER

New Materials:

- **Books**

  Alphabet Books

  ABC I Like Me! by Nancy Carlson (Puffin Books, 1999)

  Alphabet Adventure by Audrey Wood (Blue Sky Press, 2001)

  Rhyming Books

  Feast for Ten by Cathryn Falwell (Clarion Books, 1995)

  I Met a Bear by Dan Yaccarino (HarperFestival, 2002)

  The Three Bears Holiday Rhyme Book by Jane Yolen (Harcourt, 1995)

  Holiday Books

  Carl's Christmas by Alexandra Day (Farrar, Straus & Giroux, 1994)

  The Jolly Christmas Postman by Janet and Allan Ahlberg (Little, Brown and Company, 2001)

  Light the Lights!: A Story About Celebrating Hanukkah and Christmas by Margaret Moorman (Scholastic, Inc., 1999)

  My Two Grandmothers by Effin Older (Harcourt, 2000)

- **Holiday Catalogs and Newspaper Ads**

- **Props from the Class Activity "Doing the Book"**
  See *Month-by-Month Reading, Writing, and Phonics for Kindergarten* by Hall and Cunningham (Carson-Dellosa, 1997, 2003).

- **Purchased Tapes/CDs**
  Feast for Ten by Cathryn Falwell (Clarion Books, 1996)

- **Teacher-Made Tapes**
  My Two Grandmothers by Effin Older (Harcourt, 2000)

- **Sentence Strips for Interactive Charts**
  "Five Little Ducks," "Six in the Bed," "Five Green Bottles" (See page 27 for more information on interactive charts.)

- **Predictable Chart**
  "For the Holidays…" (See page 27 for more information on predictable charts.)

  - Chart with sentences
  - Cards for sentence building
  - Class book

- **Snowman Wand for Reading the Room**
  A snowman shape attached to the end of a pointer or yard stick

- **Holiday Stuffed Toys for Reading Buddies**
  Snowman, reindeer, etc.

- **Igloo Made from Empty Milk or Water Jugs for the Special Reading Place**
  See page 135 for directions.

Suggested Activities with New and Existing Materials:

Students can…

- read the books in the center to themselves or to the reading buddies, with emphasis on the new books.

- listen to the stories on tape, with emphasis on the new books.

- complete and read the interactive charts and predictable charts made during the month.

- read the room with the snowman wand. This activity can be done individually or in pairs.

- read in the Special Reading Place.

WRITING CENTER

New Materials:

- **Book**

  Carl's Christmas by Alexander Day (Farrar, Straus & Giroux, 1994)

- **December Picture Dictionary Chart from *Building-Blocks "Plus" for Kindergarten Bulletin Board* Set (Carson-Dellosa, 1998)**

  This is a chart with familiar December words and pictures such as Christmas, Hanukkah, Kwanzaa, holiday, etc.

- **Red Paper—Copy and Construction**

- **Blank Shape Books—Tree, Santa, Wreath, Candle, and Present**

  You can make the outline of the shape or you can purchase large shaped notepads from your local school supply store. You will find a candle and a present on page 136. Once you determine what shape you will use, cut blank paper to match. Each book should have 4-5 blank pages.

- **Shape Stamps—Stamps Related to Christmas, Hanukkah, and Kwanzaa**

- **Holiday Cards**

  Art Center, page 52

Suggested Activities with New and Existing Materials:

Students can…

- retell a story you have read aloud previously or a story they already know.

- make a holiday alphabet book. Encourage students to write words and draw pictures for as many letters of the alphabet as they can. You may choose to put finished books in the Reading Center.

- make holiday books. Encourage students to use words on the Picture Dictionary chart, as well as words from holiday books. You may choose to put finished books in the Reading Center.

- make a winter holiday wish list.

- interview other students in the writing center for their holiday wish list.

- make their own December picture dictionaries.

HOME LIVING CENTER

New Materials:

- **Holiday Magazines, Catalogs, Newspaper Ads**
- **Party Clothes**

Suggested Activities with New and Existing Materials:

Students can…

- plan and hold a holiday party for each other.
- take their "family" shopping for holiday gifts.

COMMUNITY CENTER

Gift Wrapping Center

New Materials:

- **Recycled Wrapping Paper**
- **Boxes of Various Sizes and Shapes**
- **Tape**
- **Bows**

- **String**
- **Ribbon**
- **Yarn**
- **Scissors**

Suggested Activities with New and Existing Materials:

Students can...

- work at the wrapping center wrapping presents.
- meet and unwrap presents as center time ends each day.

BLOCKS CENTER

New Materials:

- **Books**

    Bridges Are to Cross by Philemon Sturges (Puffin Books, 2000)

    Bridges Connect: A Building Block Book by Lee Sullivan Hill (Carolrhoda Books, 1996)

    New Road! by Gail Gibbons (Harpercollins Juvenile Books, 1983)

- **Small Model Road Signs**

    Remove at the end of the month.

- **Small Toy Cars, Trucks, and Trains**

    Remove at the end of the month.

- **Small Model Trees**

Suggested Activities with New and Existing Materials:

Students can...

- build roads. Encourage students to refer to the books in the center for construction and extension ideas.
- represent their structures on graph paper or blank paper. Post representations in the center.

SCIENCE CENTER

New Materials:

- **Plants**

    Add a plant to the center, such as ivy or any other hardy plant.

- **Magnets of Various Sizes and Shapes**
- **Metal Objects**

    Paper clips, pennies, etc.

- **Scientist's Log**

Suggested Activities with New and Existing Materials:

Students can...

- care for the new plant. They can write and post directions for taking care of the new plant.
- test and record objects that are attracted to a magnet. Students can test the walls, tables, and chairs within the Science Center. Students should record their observations in a scientist's log.
- continue to observe and care for the animals living in the Science Center.

Be sure each center has multilevel activities, a variety of materials, and oppportunities for students to interact with others.

New Materials:

- **Books**

  Feast for Ten by Cathryn Falwell (Clarion Books, 1995)

  Ten Dogs in the Window: A Countdown Book by Claire Masurel (North South Books, 1997)

- **December Pattern Cards (page 153)**
- **Variety of Holiday Candy**
- **Data for Collection and Graphing—Students' Winter Holiday Wish Lists**
- **Graph Paper**
- **Paper Clips as Uniform Units of Measure**
- **Various Objects to Measure**

Suggested Activities with New and Existing Materials:

Students can…

- make simple patterns on December Pattern Cards using connecting cubes.
- sort and classify different kinds of holiday candy by size, shape, and color.
- use the winter holiday wish lists (Writing Center, page 50) and/or re-interview students in the center to collect data and make graphs of favorite things on list.
- measure various objects using paper clips as units of measure.

ART CENTER

New Materials:

- **Books**

  Lights of Winter: Winter Celebrations Around the World by Heather Conrad (Lightport Books, 2001)

  Henri Matisse: Drawing with Scissors by Jane O'Connor (Grosset & Dunlap, 2002)

- **Sample Greeting Cards and Holiday Objects on Display**
- **Yarn or Ribbon**

Suggested Activities with New and Existing Materials:

Students can…

- create holiday cards using recyclable materials and/or paint. Encourage students to use paper and scissors with suggestions from the Matisse book.
- create holiday objects using clay. (If students make ornaments, be sure to leave a hole near the top for a loop of yarn or ribbon.) Have a place for students to lay their objects to dry. Dry objects can be painted.

> Children in literacy-enriched learning centers with adult guidance and support participate in more literacy behaviors during free time than children in thematic centers without adult guidance.

Month-by-Month Materials & Activities

| Reading | Writing | Home Living | Community | Blocks | Science | Math | Art |

READING CENTER

New Materials:

- **Books**

  Alphabet Books

  Alphabears: An ABC Book by Kathleen Hague (Henry Holt and Company, Inc., 1999)

  The Graphic Alphabet by David Pelletier (Orchard Books, 1996)

  Rhyming Books

  Five Little Monkeys Jumping on the Bed by Eileen Christelow (Scott Foresman, 1989)

  Frozen Noses by Jan Carr (Holiday House, 1999)

  Picky Mrs. Pickle by Christine M. Schneider (Walker & Company, 2001)

  Snow Dance by Lezlie Evans (Houghton Mifflin, 1997)

  Winter Books

  The Mitten by Alvin Tresselt (HarperTrophy, 1989)

  The Mitten: A Ukrainian Folktale by Jan Brett (Scholastic, Inc., 1990)

  The Old Man's Mitten: A Ukrainian Tale retold by Yevonne Pollock (Mondo Publishing, 1995)

  Snowballs by Lois Ehlert (Voyager Books, 1999)

  Time to Sleep by Denise Fleming (Henry Holt and Company, Inc., 2001)

  Winter Lullaby by Barbara Seuling (Voyager Books, 2002)

- **Props from the Class Activity "Doing the Book"**

  See *Month-by-Month Reading, Writing, and Phonics for Kindergarten* by Hall and Cunningham (Carson-Dellosa, 1997, 2003).

- **Purchased Tapes/CDs**

  Five Little Monkeys Jumping on the Bed by Eileen Christelow (Clarion Books, 1991)

- **Teacher-Made Tapes**

  The Mitten: A Ukrainian Folktale by Jan Brett (Scholastic, Inc., 1990)

- **Sentence Strips for Interactive Charts**

  "This Old Man," "One Man Went to Mow" You may want to change "mow" to a more seasonably appropriate word, such as shovel. (See page 27 for more information on interactive charts.)

- **Predictable Charts**

  "If It Snowed, I Would . . . ." (See page 27 for more information on predictable charts.)

  - Chart with sentences
  - Cards for sentence building
  - Class book

- **Shared Writing Chart**

  The Mitten: A Ukrainian Folktale by Jan Brett (Scholastic, Inc., 1990)

- **Flashlight for Reading the Room**

- **Any Stuffed Toy Animal Found in *The Mitten* for Reading Buddies**

  Mole, rabbit, hedgehog, owl, badger, fox, bear, or mouse

- **Igloo Made from Empty Milk or Water Jugs for the Special Reading Place**

  See page 135 for directions. Hang large snowflakes from the ceiling of the igloo.

- **Tongue Twisters**

Suggested Activities with New and Existing Materials:

Students can…

- read the books in the center to themselves or to the reading buddies, with emphasis on the new books.

- listen to the stories on tape, with emphasis on the new books.

- complete and read the interactive charts and predictable charts created during the month.

- read the room with the flashlight. This activity can be done individually or in pairs.

- read in the Special Reading Place.

WRITING CENTER

New Materials:

- **Books**

    From Pictures to Words: A Book About Making a Book by Janet Stevens (Holiday House, 1999)

    The Mitten by Alvin Tresselt (HarperTrophy, 1989)

    The Mitten: A Ukrainian Folktale by Jan Brett (Scholastic, Inc., 1996)

    The Old Man's Mitten: A Ukrainian Tale retold by Yevonne Pollock (Mondo Publishing, 1995)

- **January Picture Dictionary Chart from *Building-Blocks "Plus" for Kindergarten Bulletin Board* Set (Carson-Dellosa, 1998)**

    This is a chart with familiar January words and pictures such as snow, cold, winter, sled, etc.

- **Blue Paper—Copy and Construction**

- **Blank Shape Books—Snowman, Mitten, Sled, and Silhouette of Martin Luther King, Jr.**

    You can make the outline of the shape or you can purchase large shaped notepads from your local school supply store. You will find a sled on page 137. Once you determine what shape you will use, cut blank paper to match. Each book should have 4-5 blank pages.

- **Shape Stamps—Snowflakes, Snowman**

Suggested Activities with New and Existing Materials:

Students can…

- retell a story you have read aloud previously or a story they already know.

- make a winter alphabet book. Encourage students to write words and draw pictures for as many letters of the alphabet as they can. You may choose to put finished books in the Reading Center.

- make a snow book. Encourage students to use words on the Picture Dictionary chart as well as words from other winter books. You may choose to put finished books in the Reading Center.

- make a poster showing a winter activity.

HOME LIVING CENTER

New Materials:

- **Winter Magazines, Catalogs, Newspaper Ads**

- **Winter Clothes/Travel Clothes**

    Hats, scarves, gloves, etc.

- **Small Suitcases**

Suggested Activities with New and Existing Materials:

Students can…

- get dressed to play outside in the cold weather.

- pack a suitcase for a winter "vacation" to be arranged trough the Travel Agency. (Community Center, page 55)

COMMUNITY CENTER

Travel Agency

New Materials:

- **Travel Brochures**
- **Maps**
- **Books**
- **Cameras**
- **Posters**
- **Postcards**

Suggested Activities with New and Existing Materials:

Students can...

- plan and take a winter vacation. They should be able to tell where they are going, what they need to take with them, and what they plan to do when they get there.

BLOCKS CENTER

New Materials:

- **Books**

    Bear at Home by Stella Blackstone (Barefoot Books, 2001)

    Building a House by Byron Barton (William Morrow, 1981)

    Houses and Homes by Ann Morris (HarperTrophy, 1995)

    My House by Lisa Desimini (Owlet, 1997)

- **Small Toy People**
- **Small Model Trees**

    Remove at the end of the month.

Suggested Activities with New and Existing Materials:

Students can...

- build houses. Encourage students to refer to the books in the center for construction and extension ideas.
- represent their structures on graph paper or blank paper. Post representations in the center.

SCIENCE CENTER

New Materials:

- **Plants—Green Plant**

    Add another green plant to the center.

- **Animals—Crickets**

    Purchase crickets by the tube from a local bait shop. While you are there, notice the other animals that are available. These animals are not only inexpensive, they represent animals that live in the area and what students should be able to find in the their own backyards. Crickets should remain in the center for as long as possible.

- 10-20 gallon aquarium with screen lid
- Toilet paper tubes
- Cedar chips
- Dog food and apples
- Water container with cotton pad in bottom

- **Ice Cubes**
- **Balance Scale and Weights**

    For example, teddy bear weights, gram weights, etc.

Suggested Activities with New and Existing Materials:

Students can…

- care for the new plant. They can write and post directions for taking care of the new plant.

- weigh the ice cubes.

- observe the ice cubes melting. They can place three ice cubes of approximately the same size side by side and see if they all melt at about the same rate.

- observe the new animals.

- count cricket chirps.

- count cricket jumps.

- count the number of crickets on an object.

- write and post directions for taking care of the crickets.

- continue to observe and care for other plants and animals in the center.

MATH CENTER

New Materials:

- **Books**

    Five Little Monkeys Jumping on the Bed by Eileen Christelow (Scott Foresman, 1989)

    Ten Red Apples by Pat Hutchins (Greenwillow Books, 2000)

- **January Pattern Cards (page 153)**

- **Variety of Buttons**

- **Data for Collection and Graphing—Colors of Students' Winter Coat**

- **Unsharpened Pencils as Uniform Units of Measure**

- **Various Objects to Measure in Units of Unsharpened Pencils**

- **Jar Filled with Marbles**

- **Empty Jar**

    Same size and shape as the jar filled with marbles

- **Additional Marbles**

- **Box for Guesses**

    Leave in the center until the end of the year to use with other estimation activities.

Suggested Activities with New and Existing Materials:

Students can…

- make simple patterns on January pattern cards using beads and string.

- sort and classify buttons by size, shape, color, and number of buttonholes.

- ask other students in the center, "What color is your winter coat?" As a group, students in the center should collect the data and create a group graph.

- measure various objects using unsharpened pencils as units of measure and record measurements. (For example, a ruler is 1 ¾ unsharpened pencils.)

- estimate the number of marbles in the jar using the empty jar and additional marbles to assist in developing their estimation. Each student should write her name and estimate on a piece of paper, and place it in the box for guesses. When the marbles are counted at the end of the month, the class can see whose estimate came the closest.

Don't put books in centers unless you have read or discussed them. Students won't use books as references unless you have given them your "blessing."

New Materials:

Books

The First Starry Night by Joan Shaddox Isom
(Whispering Coyote Press, 2001)

I Spy: An Alphabet in Art by Lucy Micklethwait
(HarperTrophy, 1996)

Stopping by Woods on a Snowy Evening by Robert Frost
(Dutton Books, 2001)

Large Piece of Craft Paper

Hang on the wall or position on the floor in the center (if space allows).

Suggested Activities with New and Existing Materials:

Students can...

- paint and/or draw a mural with snowmen and snow scenes. Encourage students to label the pictures in the mural.

- create winter objects seen in books using recyclables materials. Display objects on a table by the mural.

Month-by-Month Materials & Activities

Reading | Writing | Home Living | Community | Blocks | Science | Math | Art

READING CENTER

New Materials:

• **Books**

   Alphabet Books

   The Alphabet Book by P. D. Eastman (Random House, 1974)

   Picture a Letter by Bradley Sneed (Phyllis Fogelman Books, 2002)

   Rhyming Books

   The Hungry Thing by Jan Slepian and Ann Seidler (Scholastic, Inc., 2001)

   The Hungry Thing Goes to a Restaurant by Jan Slepian and Ann Seidler (Scholastic, Inc., 1993)

   The Hungry Thing Returns by Jan Slepian and Ann Seidler (Scholastic, Inc., 1993)

   A Light in the Attic by Shel Silverstein (HarperCollins, 1981)

   Valentine Books

   Little Mouse's Big Valentine by Thacher Hurd (Harpercollins Juvenile Books, 1992)

   Mouse's First Valentine by Lauren Thompson (Simon & Schuster, Inc., 2002)

   One Very Best Valentine's Day by Joan W. Blos (Aladdin Library, 1998)

   Roses Are Pink, Your Feet Really Stink by Diane De Groat (HarperTrophy, 1997)

   The Valentine Bears by Eve Bunting (Clarion Books, 1985)

   Valentine Mice! by Bethany Roberts (Houghton Mifflin, 2001)

   Valentine's Day by Anne Rockwell (HarperTrophy, 2002)

• **Props from the Class Activity "Doing the Book"**
   See *Month-by-Month Reading, Writing, and Phonics for Kindergarten* by Hall and Cunningham (Carson-Dellosa, 1997, 2003).

• **Purchased Tapes/CDs**
   A Light in the Attic by Shel Silverstein (Sony Wonder, 1992)

• **Teacher-Made Tapes**
   Roses Are Pink, Your Feet Really Stink by Diane De Groat (HarperTrophy, 1997)

• **Principal-Made Tape**
   Invite your principal to read his or her favorite story aloud. Record the story as it is being read. Have students clap once when each page is turned to indicate on tape when to turn pages.

• **Sentence Strips for Interactive Charts**
   "The Flower Pot," "Mary Wore Her Red Dress," "What Is It?" (See page 27 for more information on interactive charts.)

• **Predictable Charts**
   "A is for…" (See page 27 for more information on predictable charts.)
   • Chart with sentences
   • Cards for sentence building
   • Class book

• **Heart Wand for Reading the Room**
   A heart shape with ribbon attached to the end of a pointer or yard stick

• **Valentine Stuffed Toy Animals for Reading Buddies**
   Any red or pink stuffed animals

- **Hearts of all Sizes, Shapes, and Colors for the Special Reading Place**

  Decorate the center with hearts and create a Special Reading Place.

- **Tongue Twisters**
- **Making Words Cards**

Suggested Activities with New and Existing Materials:

Students can…

- read the books in the center to themselves or to the reading buddies, with emphasis on the new books.

- listen to the stories on tape, with emphasis on the new stories.

- complete and read the interactive charts and predictable charts created during the month.

- read the room with the heart wand. This activity can be done individually or in pairs.

- read in the Special Reading Place.

- read tongue twisters to each other

- work in pairs to make words.

WRITING CENTER

New Materials:

- **Books**

  Dear Mr. Blueberry by Simon James (Aladdin Library, 1996)

  The Jolly Postman: Or Other People's Letters by Janet and Allan Ahlberg (Little, Brown and Company, 2001)

  The Post Office Book: Mail and How It Moves by Gail Gibbons (HarperTrophy, 1986)

  Toot and Puddle by Holly Hobbie (Little, Brown and Company, 1997)

- **February Picture Dictionary Chart from *Building-Blocks "Plus" for Kindergarten Bulletin Board* Set (Carson-Dellosa, 1998)**

  This is a chart with familiar February words and pictures, such as heart, valentine, Lincoln, Washington, etc.

- **Writing Paper**
- **Envelopes**
- **Postcards**
- **"Mailbox"**

  Use a decorated box with "Mail" written on it to collect the valentines and letters students make in the Writing Center.

- **Blank Shape Books—Hearts and Silhouettes of Abraham Lincoln and George Washington**

  You can make the outline of the shape or you can purchase shaped notepads from your local school supply store. You will find the Lincoln and Washington silhouettes on pages 137 and 138. Once you determine what shape you will use, cut blank paper to match. Each book should have 4-5 blank pages.

- **Shape Stamps—Hearts, Flowers**

Suggested Activities with New and Existing Materials:

Students can…

- retell a story you have read aloud previously or a story they already know.

- make valentines for their classmates or families. When valentines are completed, they should be placed in the "mailbox" for the classroom postal workers to collect, sort, and deliver.

- make a valentine book. Encourage students to use words on the Picture Dictionary chart, as well as words from other valentine books. You may choose to put finished books in the Reading Center.

- write letters or postcards to their friends. When letters or postcards are completed, they should be placed in the "mailbox" in the writing center. Classroom postal workers will collect, sort, and deliver the letters.

- make a February picture dictionary.

New Materials:

- **Valentine's Day Magazines, Catalogs, Newspaper Ads**

- **Boxes of Various Shapes and Sizes**

- **Address Labels—4.25" x 5.5" (108 mm x 139.5 mm)**
  ¼ sheets of copy paper

Suggested Activities with New and Existing Materials:
Students can…

- plan and have a valentine party for each other.

- prepare valentine packages for mailing to family or friends. Packages should be labeled for delivery.

COMMUNITY CENTER

Post Office

New Materials:

- **Postal Worker Clothes**
  Blue shirts, blue socks, blue hats, etc.

- **Letters**
  Writing Center, page 59

- **Postcards**
  Writing Center, page 59

- **Packages**

- **Valentines**
  Art Center, page 62

- **Student Mailboxes**

Suggested Activities with New and Existing Materials:
Students can…

- sort and deliver valentines to classmates.

- deliver packages back to the Home Living Center.

BLOCKS CENTER

New Materials:

- **Books**
  Alphabet City by Stephen T. Johnson (Puffin Books, 1999)

  Block City by Robert Louis Stevenson (Puffin Books, 1992)

  City: A Story of Roman Planning and Construction by David MacAulay (Houghton Mifflin/Walter Lorraine Books, 1983)

  Roxaboxen by Barbara Cooney (HarperCollins, 1991)

- **Small Toy Cars, Trucks, and Trains**
  Remove at the end of the month.

- **Small Toy People**
  Remove at the end of the month.

Suggested Activities with New and Existing Materials:
Students can…

- build a city (or cities). Encourage students to refer to the books in the center for construction and extension ideas.

- represent their structures on graph paper or blank paper. Post representations in the center.

New Materials:

• Plants

Add a blooming plant to the center.

• Animals—Worms

Purchase worms from a local bait shop. There are two different kinds of worms found in most bait shops. If you can get red wrigglers they will decompose raw fruits and vegetables. Night crawlers do not decompose; they only dig holes to aerate the soil. Worms can also be purchased on-line. Worms should remain in the center for as long as possible.

- Any large container (preferably one that is clear so students can observe the worms in the soil)
- Dirt/potting soil
- Hand sprayer/mister
- Raw fruits and vegetables (if using red wrigglers)
- Large wooden spoons
- Paper plates

Suggested Activities with New and Existing Materials:

Students can…

- care for the new plant. They can write and post directions for taking care of the new plant. They can make a poster identifying how this plant is like the other plants and how it is different.
- continue to observe and care for other plants and animals in center.
- write and post directions for taking care of the worms.
- observe the worms.

If you get red wrigglers, students can:

- feed the worms leftovers from lunch (no meat— fruits, vegetables, bread, rice, etc.). See how long it takes to decompose an apple, a banana peel, a raw carrot stick, etc.
- count the number of worms on any piece of fruit or vegetable.

If you get night crawlers, students can:

- Take one worm out and measure how long it is.
- See how many worms you can dig up with one spoonful of dirt.

New Materials:

• Book

Dogs, Dogs, Dogs! by Leslea Newman (Simon & Schuster, Inc., 2002)

The Water Hole by Graeme Base (Abrams Books for Young Readers, 2001)

• February Pattern Cards (pages 154-158)
• Candy Conversation Hearts
• Rulers
• Various Objects to Measure
• Jar Filled with Cotton Balls
• Empty Jar

Same size and shape as the jar filled with cotton balls

• Bag of Cotton Balls

Suggested Activities with New and Existing Materials:

Students can…

- make more complex patterns on February pattern cards using pattern blocks.
- sort and classify candy conversation hearts by color, number of letters, number of words.
- measure and record measurements of various objects using a ruler.
- estimate the number of cotton balls in the jar using the empty jar and additional cotton balls to assist in developing their estimate. Each student should write his estimate and name on a piece of paper and place it in the box for guesses (added to the center in January). When the cotton balls are counted at the end of the month, the class can see whose estimate came the closest.

New Materials:

- **Books**

    A Is for Artist: A Getty Museum Alphabet by John Harris (J. Paul Getty Museum Publications, 1997)

    Edgar Degas: Paintings That Dance by Maryann Cocca-Leffler (Grossett & Dunlap, 2001)

- **"Mailbox"**

    Use a decorated box with "Mail" written on it to collect the valentines students make in the center.

- **Old Valentines**

Suggested Activities with New and Existing Materials:

Students can…

- make valentine boxes using old valentines and other recyclable materials. Have students write the directions for making their boxes.

- paint and/or draw a valentine. When it is completed, students can write a greeting inside. If they want the valentine to be delivered to someone in class, they can write that persons name on it and place it in the mailbox in the center.

Glue comes in many different forms. Instead of white glue, try glitter glue, colored glue, 3-D glue, or glue sticks to create some fun effects and decorations.

Month-by-Month Materials & Activities

| Reading | Writing | Home Living | Community | Blocks | Science | Math | Art |

READING CENTER

New Materials:

- **Books**

    Alphabet Books

    Animal ABC by David Wojtowycz (Sterling, 2000)

    Ape in a Cape: An Alphabet of Odd Animals by Fritz Eichenberg (Voyager Books, 1989)

    Miss Spider's ABC by David Kirk (Callaway Editions, 1998)

    Rhyming Books

    How Do Dinosaurs Say Good Night? by Jane Yolen (Blue Sky Press, 2000)

    Is Your Mama a Llama? by Deborah Guarino (Scholastic, Inc., 1991)

    St. Patrick's Day and Windy Books

    Gilberto and the Wind by Marie Hall Ets (Puffin Books, 1978)

    How Does the Wind Walk? by Nancy White Carlstrom (Simon & Schuster, Inc., 1993)

    If I Were the Wind by Lezlie Evans (Eager Minds Press, 2001)

    Kite Flying by Grace Lin (Random House, 2002)

    St. Patrick's Day in the Morning by Eve Bunting (Clarion Books, 1983)

    What Will the Weather Be Like? by Paul Rogers (Scholastic Paperbacks, 1992)

    When the Wind Stops by Charlotte Zolotow (HarperTrophy, 1997)

    The Wind Blew by Pat Hutchins (Aladdin Library, 1993)

- **Props from the Class Activity "Doing the Book"**

    See *Month-by-Month Reading, Writing, and Phonics for Kindergarten* by Hall and Cunningham (Carson-Dellosa, 1997, 2003).

- **Purchased Tapes/CDs**

    St. Patrick's Day in the Morning by Eve Bunting (Clarion Books, 2001)

- **Teacher-Made Tapes**

    The Wind Blew by Pat Hutchins (Aladdin Library, 1993)

- **Blank Tapes for Student Reading**

- **Buddy-Made Tapes**

    Invite older readers from your "buddy room" to record a story. Add recorded stories to the Reading Center.

- **Sentence Strips for Interactive Charts**

    "Crayons," "Teddy Bear," "Oh, A-Hunting We Will Go" (See page 27 for more information on interactive charts.)

- **Predictable Charts**

    "The Wind Blew" and "A Kite Story" (See page 27 for more information on predictable charts.)

    - Charts with sentences
    - Cards for sentence building
    - Class book

- **Kite Wand for Reading the Room**

    A kite shape attached to the end of a pointer or yard stick

- **Stuffed Toy Lions and Lambs for Reading Buddies**

- **Large Kite for the Special Reading Place**

    Hang the kite over one section of the center. If possible hang the kite rather low so it feels as if students are reading under it.

- **Tongue Twisters**

- **Making Words Cards**

Suggested Activities with New and Existing Materials:

Students can...

- read the books in the center to themselves or to the reading buddies, with emphasis on the new books.

- listen to the stories on tape, with emphasis on the new stories.

- read a favorite story aloud and make a tape recording.

- complete and read the interactive charts and predictable charts made during the month.

- read the room with the kite wand. This activity can be done individually or in pairs.

- read in the Special Reading Place.

- read tongue twisters to each other

- work in pairs to make words.

WRITING CENTER

New Materials:

- **Books**

    Aunt Isabel Tells a Good One by Kate Duke (Puffin Books, 1994)

    How Does the Wind Walk? by Nancy White Carlstrom (Simon & Schuster, Inc., 1993)

    If I Were the Wind by Lezlie Evans (Eager Minds Press, 2001)

    Where Does the Wind Blow? by Cynthia A. Rink (Dawn Publications, 2002)

- **March Picture Dictionary Chart from *Building-Blocks "Plus" for Kindergarten Bulletin Board* Set (Carson-Dellosa, 1998)**

    This is a chart with familiar March words and pictures such as wind, kite, leprechaun, shamrock, etc.

- **Chart with Student Names and Phone Numbers**

    Ask parent(s) for permission to post and share home phone numbers with class members before beginning this activity.

- **Yellow Paper—Copy and Construction**

- **Blank Shape Books—Lion, Lamb, and Shamrock**

    You can make the outline of the shape or you can purchase large shaped notepads from your local school supply store. Once you determine what shape you will use, cut blank paper to match. Each book should have 4-5 blank pages.

- **Shape Stamps—School-Related Shapes**

    Schoolhouse, bus, pencils, books, etc.

- **Clipboards**

    Clipboards remain in the center for the rest of the year.

Suggested Activities with New and Existing Materials:

Students can...

- retell a story you have read aloud previously or a story they already know. Completed stories may be placed in the Reading Center.

- make a class phone book. A Name, phone number, and picture for each child will complete the phone book. Students will need to use the name board and phone number chart to complete the activity. Completed phone books can be placed in the Home Living Center.

- make a poster advertising the kites they made in the Art Center (page 67).

- make a March picture dictionary.

- use the clipboards and blank paper to write the room.

Invite children to plan a center (or several centers) with you. Tell them the theme or the month of study, and ask them what activities and materials could be included.

HOME LIVING CENTER

New Materials:

- **Magazines, Catalogs, Newspaper Ads with a Variety of Medications**
- **4.25" x 5.5" (108 mm x 139.5 mm) Pieces of Paper**
  ¼ sheets of copy paper
- **Scissors**
- **Glue**
- **Doctor/Nurse Clothing**

Suggested Activities with New and Existing Materials:

Students can…

- find pictures of medications in the magazines, catalogs, and newspaper ads. Students should cut out the pictures, glue them on index size pieces of paper, and write the name of the medications to make coupons. The coupons should be stored until the grocery store is opened in April (page 70).

Children need 20-30 minute play sessions to create elaborate scripts that lead to the intentional use of literacy in dramatic play.

COMMUNITY CENTER

Hospital/Doctor's Office

New Materials:
- **Telephone**
- **Message Pad**
- **Appointment Book**
- **Stethoscope**
- **Thermometer**
- **Tongue Depressors**
- **Bandages**
- **Stickers**

Suggested Activities with New and Existing Materials:

Students can…

- take a "sick child" to the doctor. A receptionist should take appointments and check in patients. A "nurse" should check weight and height. A "doctor" should record how the child is feeling and write a prescription. The nurse can "fill" the prescription. Sick children should be given a sticker when they leave.

BLOCKS CENTER

New Materials:

- **Book**
  Castle by David MacAulay (Houghton Mifflin/ Walter Lorraine Books, 1982)

Suggested Activities with New and Existing Materials:

Students can…

- build a castle(s). Encourage students to refer to the book in the center for construction and extension ideas.
- represent their structures on graph paper or blank paper. Post representations in the center.

New Materials:

• **Book**

A Salamander's Life by John Himmelman (Children's Book Press, 1998)

• **Plants**

Add a shamrock plant (or look alike).

• **Animals—Mudpuppy (Salamander)**

Purchase a mudpuppy at a local bait shop or pet store. Mudpuppy is the common term for an aquatic animal that looks like a large tadpole with legs and frilly gills. The term mudpuppy, or "water dog," is broadly used for various types of salamanders. The mudpuppy you find may be a mudpuppy, an axolotl, or a larval (tadpole stage) tiger salamander. Mudpuppies and axolotls retain their gills for their entire lives. Larval tiger salamanders will transform, like all larval stage animals, into adult tiger salamanders, losing their gills and tails. In all species, watch for changes in gills and general activity level. These may be indicators of transformation or a need to clean or add water.

The mudpuppy can live in a small aquarium filled about ¾ full. It likes to hide so arrange rocks in the bottom with areas where they can hide. The mudpuppy is a hearty animal and should remain in the center for the rest of the school year.

If your mudpuppy is a larval salamander, it may not transform during the school year. If it does, the aquarium needs to also transform. Significantly reduce the amount of water to create an aqua-terrarium. Leave a shallow amount of water (1-2"/ 2.5-5 cm) in the bottom with plenty of rocks, soil, or peat. Half of the aqua-terrarium should allow the salamander access to water, the other half to dry land.

It is a good idea to get additional information by searching the Internet or purchasing a book on mudpuppies and salamanders.

• 10-20 gallon aquarium
• Rocks
• Food (brine shrimp, tubifex worm cubes, food sticks, or pellets)

Suggested Activities with New and Existing Materials:

Students can…

• care for the new plant. Students can write and post directions for taking care of the new plant. They should make a poster identifying how this plant is like the other plants and how it is different.

• observe the mudpuppy. Encourage students to use the resources in the center as they observe the mudpuppy. Some questions to guide observations: How does the mudpuppy spend most of its time? How does the mudpuppy look like a tadpole? How is it different? Does it remind young scientists of anything else?

• write and post directions for taking care of the mudpuppy.

• continue to observe and care for the other plants and animals in the center.

New Materials:

• **Books**

How Many Bugs in a Box? by David A. Carter (Little Simon, 1988)

Ten Little Ladybugs by Melanie Gerth (Piggy Toes Press, 2001)

• **March Pattern Cards (page 159)**
• **Rocks of Various Sizes, Shapes, and Colors**

• **Yardsticks**
• **Masking Tape**
• **Various Objects to Measure**
• **Rocks of Similar Size and Shape**
  Such as pea gravel
• **Jar Filled with Rocks of Similar Size and Shape**

Suggested Activities with New and Existing Materials:

Students can...

- make more complex patterns on March activity cards using pattern cubes.

- sort and classify rocks by size, shape, color, and hardness.

- measure various pieces of furniture, objects, masking tape lines on the floor, and each other with yardsticks. They should record what objects they measured and their measurements.

- estimate the number of rocks in the jar using the additional rocks to assist in developing their estimate (without using another empty jar for support). Each student should write her name and estimate on a piece of paper and place it in the box for guesses (added to the center in January). When the rocks are counted at the end of the month, the class can see whose estimate came the closest.

ART CENTER

New Materials:

- **Books**

  An Island in the Sun by Stella Blackstone (Barefoot Books, 2003)

  How Artists See The Weather by Colleen Carroll (Abbeville Press, Inc., 1998)

- **Tissue Paper**
- **Wrapping Paper**
- **Newspaper**
- **Craft Sticks**

Suggested Activities with New and Existing Materials:

Students can...

- use paper and craft sticks to make kites. Students may decorate their kites with recyclable items.

- paint and/or draw children and glue their kites on the page.

- paint and/or draw various scenes with weather. Encourage children to refer to the books in the center.

Learning centers that provide choice, control, and appropriate levels of challenge appear to facilitate the development of self-regulated, intentional learning in students.

Month-by-Month Materials & Activities

Reading | Writing | Home Living | Community | Blocks | Science | Math | Art

READING CENTER

New Materials:

- **Books**

  Alphabet Books

  The ABC Exhibit by Leonard Fisher (Atheneum, 1991)

  The Z Was Zapped: A Play in Twenty-Six Acts by Chris Van Allsburg (Houghton Mifflin, 1998)

  Rhyming Books

  The Piggy in the Puddle by Charlotte Pomerantz (Aladdin Library, 1989)

  Rain Song by Lezlie Evans (Houghton Mifflin, 1997)

  Rain and Flower Books

  Planting a Rainbow by Lois Ehlert (Voyager Books, 1992)

  Rain by Manya Stojic (Chrysalis Books, 2000)

  Red Rubber Boot Day by Mary Lyn Ray (Harcourt, 2000)

  The Rose in My Garden by Arnold Lobel (HarperTrophy, 1993)

  Water Dance by Thomas Locker (Voyager Books, 2002)

  The Wind's Garden by Bethany Roberts (Bill Martin Books, 2001)

- **Props from the Class Activity "Doing the Book"**
  See *Month-by-Month Reading, Writing, and Phonics for Kindergarten* by Hall and Cunningham (Carson-Dellosa, 1997, 2003).

- **Teacher-Made Tapes**
  Planting a Rainbow by Lois Ehlert (Voyager Books, 1992)

- **Blank Tapes for Student Reading**

- **Sentence Strips for Interactive Charts**
  "Down in the Meadow," "Chickadee" (See page 27 for more information on interactive charts.)

- **Predictable Chart**
  "Where Does the Butterfly Go When It Rains?" (See page 27 for more information on predictable charts.)
  - Chart with sentences
  - Cards for sentence building
  - Class book

- **Flower Wand for Reading the Room**
  An artificial flower attached to the end of a pointer or yard stick

- **Rainy Day Stuffed Toy Shapes for Reading Buddies**
  Plants, raindrops, rainbows, etc.

- **Large Umbrella for the Special Reading Place**
  Hang the umbrella over a part of the Reading Center. If possible hang it rather low so students feel like they are reading under the umbrella.

- **Tongue Twisters**

- **Making Words Cards**

- **Environmental Print—Cereal Boxes**

- **Letter Cards to Spell Cereal Names**

Suggested Activities with New and Existing Materials:

Students can…

- read the books in the center to themselves or to the reading buddies, with emphasis on the new books.

- listen to the stories on tape, with emphasis on the new stories.

- record tapes of themselves reading favorite stories aloud.
- complete and read the interactive charts and predictable charts created during the month.
- read the room with the flower wand. This activity can be done individually or in pairs.

- read in the Special Reading Place.
- read tongue twisters to each other.
- work in pairs to make words.
- use letter cards to make words found on the environmental print board.

WRITING CENTER

New Materials:

- **Books**

    Red Rubber Boot Day by Mary Lyn Ray (Harcourt, 2000)

    The Rose in My Garden by Arnold Lobel (HarperTrophy, 1993)

    Simon's Book by Henrick Drescher (Harpercollins Children's Books, 1983)

    Water Dance by Thomas Locker (Voyager Books, 2002)

- **April and May Picture Dictionary Chart from *Building-Blocks "Plus" for Kindergarten Bulletin Board* Set (Carson-Dellosa, 1998)**

    This is a chart with familiar April words and pictures such as rain, flowers, eggs, basket, etc.

- **Green Paper—Copy and Construction**
- **Blank Shape Books—Flowers, Flowerpot, Umbrella, and Rainbow**

    You can make the outline of the shape or you can purchase large shaped notepads from your local school supply store. A rainbow shape can be found on page 146. Once you determine what shape you will use, cut blank paper to match. Each book should have 4-5 blank pages.

- **Shape Stamps—Flowers, Rainbows**

Suggested Activities with New and Existing Materials:

Students can...

- retell a story you have read aloud previously or a story they already know. Completed stories may be placed in the Reading Center.
- write stories about something special that happened during this school year. Encourage students to use resources posted around the room, books in the Reading Center, and any other resources to write their books.
- write directions for completing an activity in another center. This can be done on poster board or on writing paper. When the directions are completed students may post them in the appropriate center.
- make April picture dictionaries.
- continue to write the room.

HOME LIVING CENTER

New Materials:
- **Spring and Gardening Magazines, Catalogs, and Newspaper Ads**
- **Gardening Clothes and Tools**
- **Gloves**
- **Knee Pads**

- **Hats**
- **Flower Pots**
- **Shovels**
- **Buckets**
- **Plastic/Cloth Flowers**

Suggested Activities with New and Existing Materials:

Students can…

- begin a home "garden." Mark off a section of the center with masking tape. Use the tape to create rows for a garden to be planted.

- find pictures of gardening supplies in the magazines, catalogs, and newspaper ads. Students should cut out the pictures, glue them on index size pieces of paper, and write the names of the supplies to make coupons.

COMMUNITY CENTER

Grocery Store

New Materials:

- **Food**
  - Boxes
  - Cans
  - Bags
- **Grocery Bags—Paper and Plastic**
- **Paper for Grocery Lists and Receipts**
- **Carts or Baskets**
- **Gardening Supplies**

Suggested Activities with New and Existing Materials:

Students can…

- go to the grocery store to buy food, medication, and gardening supplies. Encourage students to use the coupons made this month and those made last month.

BLOCKS CENTER

New Materials:

- **Book**

  Cathedral: The Story of Its Construction by David MacAulay (Houghton Mifflin/Walter Lorraine Books, 1981)

- **Small Toy Cars, Trucks, and Trains**

  Remove at the end of the month.

- **Small Model Trees**

  Remove at the end of the month.

Suggested Activities with New and Existing Materials:

Students can…

- build a cathedral or other ornate building. Encourage students to refer to the books in the center for construction and extension ideas.

- represent their structures on graph paper or blank paper. Post representations in the center.

SCIENCE CENTER

New Materials:

- **Plants—Seeds**

  Any type of seed will work well. Check with the local garden center for a plant that will grow well in your area when planted outside in the spring.

- **Cups—Plastic or Foam**
- **Dirt/Potting Soil**
- **Plastic Tablecloth**

- **Plastic Spoons**
- **Watering Can**
- **Craft Sticks**
- **Pieces of Paper about the Size of a Seed Packet**
- **Empty Seed Packets as Examples**
- **Markers**
- **Glue**

Suggested Activities with New and Existing Materials:

Students can…

- decorate cups for their new plants. They may use the markers or any other materials available.

- plant the seeds in their newly decorated cups. Encourage students to work on the plastic tablecloth and keep the dirt and watering can in that space.

  Note: Students should need minimal supervision with this activity. Although the dirt might be a bit messy, there is nothing in the dirt that can harm children or damage other materials.

- make name cards for their plants. These names card should tell who planted the seed, what kind of seed it is, and how to care for the plant. They should create a "seed packet" with the necessary information. Seed packets can be glued to craft sticks and placed in the plants.

- take their plants home at the end of the month or plant them in a garden at school.

- continue to observe and care for the plants and animals in the center.

MATH CENTER

New Materials:

- **Books**

  Gray Rabbit's 1, 2, 3 by Alan Baker (Larousse Kingfisher Chambers, 1999)

  Ten Sly Piranhas: A Counting Story in Reverse by William Wise (Dial Books, 1993)

- **Fruit-Flavored Ring Cereal**

  Rings should be a variety of colors.

- **String**

- **Data for Collection and Graphing—Students' Favorite Foods**

- **Cup, Pint, and Quart Measures (250 ml, 500 ml, 1 L)**

  Empty milk containers will work well.

- **Pitchers of Water**

- **Large Tub**

  To catch water as it is being measured

- **Jar Filled with Colorful Candy-Covered Chocolates**

Suggested Activities with New and Existing Materials:

Students can…

- make more complex patterns using fruit-flavored ring cereal and string.

- record their patterns and challenge other students to create the same patterns they did.

- sort and classify pattern blocks by size, shape, and color.

- interview the other students in the center to determine their favorite foods. Students should make a graph of these favorite foods.

- determine how many cups (250 ml containers) are in a pint (500 ml container), how many cups (250 ml containers) are in a quart (1 L container), and how many pints (500 ml containers) are in a quart (1 L container) by pouring water from pitchers into measuring containers. Students should record equivalent measures.

- estimate the number of colorful candy-covered chocolates in the jar without any additional support. Each student should write her name and estimate on a piece of paper and place it in the box for guesses (added to the center in January). When the colorful candy-covered chocolates are counted at the end of the month, the class can see whose estimate came the closest.

New Materials:

- **Books**

  I Spy Two Eyes: Numbers in Art by Lucy Micklethwait (Mulberry Books, 1998)

  North Country Spring by Reeve Lindbergh (Houghton Mifflin, 1997)

- **Watercolor Paints**

Suggested Activities with New and Existing Materials:

Students can…

- make umbrellas using recyclables materials. Have students write the directions for making their umbrellas.

- draw and paint rainy scenes using watercolors. Encourage students to label their pictures.

Interaction with an adult during center time is a critical contributor to student development.

Month-by-Month Materials & Activities

Reading | **Writing** | **Home Living** | **Community** | **Blocks** | **Science** | **Math** | **Art**

READING CENTER

New Materials:

- **Books**

  Alphabet Books

  The Butterfly Alphabet by Kjell Sandved (Scholastic, Inc., 1996)

  Summer: An Alphabet Acrostic by Steven Schnur (Clarion Books, 2001)

  Rhyming Books

  Beach Day by Karen Roosa (Clarion Books, 2001)

  Down By the Cool of the Pool by Tony Mitton (The Watts Publishing Group, 2002)

  Summersaults: Poems & Paintings by Douglas Florian (Greenwillow Books, 2002)

  Summer Books

  The Berenstain Bears Go to Camp by Stan and Jan Berenstain (Random House, 1982)

  Cool Ali by Nancy Poydar (Margaret K. McElderry Books 1996)

  Marshmallow Kisses by Linda Crotta Brennan (Houghton Mifflin, 2000)

  Milly and Tilly: The Story of a Town Mouse and a Country Mouse by Kate Summers (Puffin Books, 2000)

  On the Go by Ann Morris (HarperTrophy, 1994)

  Summer Stinks by Marty Kelley (Zino Press Children's Books, 2001)

- **Props from the Class Activity "Doing the Book"**
  See *Month-by-Month Reading, Writing, and Phonics for Kindergarten* by Hall and Cunningham (Carson-Dellosa, 1997, 2003).

- **Teacher-Made Tape**
  Milly and Tilly: The Story of a Town Mouse and a Country Mouse by Kate Summers (Puffin Books, 2000)

- **Blank Tapes for Student Reading**

- **Sentence Strips for Interactive Charts**
  "This is the Way," "Roses are Red" (See page 27 for more information on interactive charts.)

- **Predictable Charts**
  "Happy Mother's Day" (See page 27 for more information on predictable charts.)
  - Chart with Sentences
  - Cards for Sentence Building
  - Class Book

- **Poetry**
  - Charts
  - Jump Rope Rhymes ("A My Name is Alice," "Teddy Bear Teddy Bear," "Miss Mary Mack")

- **Inexpensive Sunglasses for Reading the Room**

- **Any Stuffed Toy Animals Wearing Bathing Suits or Other Summer Clothes for Reading Buddies**

- **A Small Child's Wading Pool with Pillows for the Special Reading Place**

- **Tongue Twisters**

- **Making Words Cards**

- **Environmental Print—Restaurants**
  Bags, boxes, cups, etc. with restaurant logos and names

- **Letter Cards to Spell Restaurant Names**

Suggested Activities with New and Existing Materials:

Students can...

- read the books in the center to themselves or to the reading buddies, with emphasis on the new books.

- listen to the stories on tape, with emphasis on the new stories.

- make a tape recording as they read a favorite story aloud.

- complete and read the interactive charts and predictable charts made during the month.

- read the room with the sunglasses. Students wear sunglasses to read the room. They may carry a pointer or yardstick. This activity can be done individually or in pairs.

- read in the Special Reading Place.

- read tongue twisters to each other.

- work in pairs to make words.

- use letter cards to make words found on the restaurant environmental print board.

WRITING CENTER

New Materials:

- **Books**

    Cookbooks—both adult's and children's

    The Berenstain Bears Go to Camp by Stan and Jan Berenstain (Random House, 1982)

    On the Go by Ann Morris (HarperTrophy, 1994)

    My Duck by Tanya Linch (Bloomsbury Publishing, 2001)

- **Magazines and Catalogs for Cutting out Pictures**

- **April/May Picture Dictionary Chart from *Building-Blocks "Plus" for Kindergarten Bulletin Board* Set (Carson-Dellosa, 1998)**

    This is a chart with familiar May words and pictures such as Mother's Day, flower, umbrella, etc.

- **Goldenrod Paper—Copy and Construction**

- **Blank Picture Dictionary Books**

    Make picture dictionaries from construction paper and blank paper. Each picture dictionary should have 13 pages, one for each letter of the alphabet (front and back).

- **Blank Cookbooks**

    Make cookbooks from construction paper and blank paper. Each cookbook should have 5-6 blank pages.

- **Paper for Class Newspaper**

- **Shape Stamps—Summer Objects**

    Sun, swimming pool, bathing suit, etc.

Suggested Activities with New and Existing Materials:

Students can...

- retell a story you have read aloud previously or a story they already know. Completed stories may be placed in the Reading Center.

- make a picture dictionary with a picture(s) for each letter of the alphabet. Students may choose to draw a picture for each letter or cut out a picture from the available magazines and catalogs. It may take students several days to complete their picture dictionaries. Have a place for them to be stored between visits to the center.

- make a cookbook of their favorite things to eat. Encourage students to see how cookbooks are organized.

- make a class newspaper. Reporters should interview other students in the center about their favorite things in kindergarten. Then, the reporters write "articles" for the teacher to type. Save the newspapers to share and take home at end of year.

- continue to write the room.

HOME LIVING CENTER

New Materials:

- **Summer Magazines, Catalogs, and Newspaper Ads**
- **Shorts, T-Shirts, Swim Suit Wraps, Sunscreen, Beach Towels, and Beach Bags**

Suggested Activities with New and Existing Materials:

Students can...

- plan family summer outings using ideas from magazines, catalogs, and newspaper ads.
- make plans to take the "family" swimming. They should pack clothing and other supplies to take the pool, ocean, or lake.

COMMUNITY CENTER

Restaurant

New Materials:

- **Table**
- **Chair**
- **Tablecloth**
- **Menus**
- **Plates**
- **Napkins**
- **Silverware**
- **Glasses**
- **Food**

Suggested Activities with New and Existing Materials:

Students can...

- work at and visit the restaurant. Restaurateurs should make menus of what is to be served each day, set the tables, and serve food to the guests.

> Be creative about finding materials. Post a learning centers wish list in the hall outside your classroom door. Don't forget to ask parents and other teachers to help.

BLOCKS CENTER

New Materials:

Plastic Interlocking Blocks

Suggested Activities with New and Existing Materials:

Students can...

- build a structure or object using the plastic interlocking blocks. Encourage students to refer to the books in the center for construction and extension ideas.
- represent their structures on graph paper or blank paper. Post representations in the center.

New Materials:

- **Plants—Blooming Plant**
  Add a blooming plant to the center.

- **Thermometer**

- **Weather Chart**

Suggested Activities with New and Existing Materials:

Students can...

- care for the new plant. They can write and post directions for taking care of the new plant. They should make a poster identifying how this plant is like the other plants and how it is different.

- read the thermometer and record the daily temperature on a chart in the center.

- record weather conditions (for example, cloudy, sunny, etc.) on the chart.

- continue to observe and care for the plants and animals in center.

- dispose of the log and release the insects, crickets, mudpuppy (near a creek or river), and worms on the last day of school. The mammal and fish may be sent home with a chosen student on the last day.

MATH CENTER

New Materials:

- **Books**
  Ten, Nine, Eight by Molly Garret Bang (HarperTrophy, 1991)

  The Baseball Counting Book by Barbara McGrath (Charlesbridge Publishing, 1999)

- **Keys of Various Sizes, Shapes, and Colors**
- **Data for Collection and Graphing—Students' Favorite Restaurants**
- **Measuring Spoons**
- **Measuring Cups**
- **Pitchers of Water**
- **Large Tub**
- **Jar Filled with Jelly Beans**

Suggested Activities with New and Existing Materials:

Students can...

- make more complex patterns with keys. Have students record their patterns.

- sort and classify keys by size, shape, and color.

- interview the other students in the center to determine their favorite restaurants. Students should make a graph of their favorite restaurants.

- determine how many tablespoons (15 ml measures) and teaspoons (5 ml measures) are in ¼ cup (60 ml measure), ½ cup (120 ml measure), and a cup (240 ml measure). Students should record equivalent measures.

- estimate the number of jellybeans in the jar. Each student should write her name and estimate on a piece of paper and place it in the box for guesses (added to the center in January). When the jelly beans are counted at the end of the month, the class can see whose estimate came the closest.

Place special writing tools in centers to get students excited about writing. Consider placing interesting pencils or fine-tip markers with writing paper and encourage students to write with the new tools.

New Materials:

• **Books**

Little Green by Keith Baker (Harcourt, 2001)

Squeaking of Art: The Mice Go to the Museum by Monica Wellington (Dutton Books, 2000)

• **Large Piece of Craft Paper**

Suggested Activities with New and Existing Materials:

Students can…

• make flowers using recyclables materials. Have students write the directions for making their flowers.

• paint and/or draw flowers. Encourage students to use the resources in the center as they make their flowers.

• create a spring mural with the craft paper and the paper flowers made in Art Center. Encourage students to label their work on the mural.

Theme Materials & Activities

Themes may last for two to four weeks. You may choose to have some theme centers, as well as some month-by-month centers.

Reading | Writing | Home Living | Community | Blocks | Science | Math | Art

---

READING CENTER

New Materials:

- **Books**

  The Adventures of a Nose by Viviane Schwartz (Candlewick Press, 2002)

  Eyes, Nose, Fingers, and Toes by Judy Hindley (Candlewick Press, 2002)

  The Foot Book by Dr. Seuss (Random House, 1968)

  I Like Me by Nancy Carlson (Pearson Learning, 1990)

  More Parts by Tedd Arnold (Dial Books for Young Readers, 2001)

  My Feet by Aliki (Harpercollins Juvenile Books, 1992)

  My Five Senses by Aliki (HarperCollins, 1989)

  My Hands by Aliki (Harpercollins Juvenile Books, 1992)

  On the Day You Were Born by Debra Frasier (Harcourt, 1995)

  Peter's Chair by Ezra Jack Keats (Puffin Books, 1998)

  Smile a Lot by Nancy Carlson (Carolrhoda Books, Inc., 2002)

  This Is My Body by Mercer Mayer (Golden Books Publishing Company, Inc., 2000)

- **Purchased Tapes/CDs**

  On the Day You Were Born by Debra Frasier (Harcourt Young Classics, 1992)

- **Teacher-Made Tapes**

  Any students' "All about Me" (taped while being read)

- **Mirror Wand for Reading the Room**

  An aluminum foil mirror in a construction paper frame attached to a pointer or yardstick

- **Sentence Strips for Interactive Charts**

  "Me," "My Body," "Clothing" (See page 27 for more information on interactive charts.)

- **Predictable Charts**

  "I Can . . . ," "Things I Like To Do," "Things I Do Not Like to Do," "Me" (See page 27 for more information on predictable charts.)

  - Charts with sentences
  - Cards for sentence building
  - Class books

- **Children's Favorite Stuffed Toy Animals or Dolls from Home for Reading Buddies**

- **"Throne" for the Special Reading Place**

  Decorate a comfortable chair to be the "throne" for the Special Reading Place. Provide a crown for each student to wear while she is reading on the throne.

Suggested Activities with New and Existing Materials:

Students can...

- read the books in the center to themselves or to the reading buddies, with emphasis on "all about me" books.

- listen to the stories on tape, with emphasis on "all about me" stories.

- complete and read the theme related interactive charts and predictable charts made during the All about Me unit.

- read the room with the mirror. This activity can be done individually or in pairs.

- read in the Special Reading Place.

New Materials:

- **Books**

  Toot and Puddle by Holly Hobbie (Little, Brown and Company, 1997)

- **All about Me Picture Dictionary Chart**

  This is a chart with familiar "me" words and pictures such as me, head, eyes, ears, hands, feet, toes, shirt, shoes, heart, bones, etc.

- **Face Shape Books**

  You will find the shapes of a boy child's head and a girl child's head on pages 138 and 139. You will need to cut blank paper to match. Each book should have 4-5 blank pages.

- **Shape Stamps—Parts of the Body**

  Hands, feet, eyes, etc.

- **Clipboard**

Suggested Activities with New and Existing Materials:

Students can…

- write retellings of "All about Me" stories you have read aloud previously or stories they already know. Completed stories may be placed in the Reading Center.

- make "All about Me" picture dictionaries.

- write the room.

HOME LIVING CENTER

New Materials:

- **Blank "Photo Albums"**
- **4.25" x 5.5" (108 mm x 139.5 mm) Pieces of Paper—"Photo" Paper**
- **Markers**
- **Glue**
- **Tape**
- **Magazines**
- **Hanging Mirror**

Suggested Activities with New and Existing Materials:

Students can…

- make photo albums of themselves doing things they have done and like to do. Students will cut out pictures from magazines and draw themselves in the pictures. Then, they will glue the pictures to "photo" paper and tape them in photo albums.

COMMUNITY CENTER

Hospital/Doctor's Office

New Materials:

- **Telephone**
- **Message Pad**
- **Appointment Book**
- **Stethoscope**
- **Thermometer**
- **Tongue Depressors**
- **Bandages**
- **Stickers**

Suggested Activities with New and Existing Materials:

Students can…

- take a "sick child" to the doctor. A "receptionist" should take appointments and check in patients. A "nurse" should check patients' weight and height. A "doctor" should record how the child is feeling and write a prescription. The nurse can "fill" the prescription. Patients should be given a sticker when they leave.

BLOCKS CENTER

New Materials:

Books

Nora's Room by Jessica Harper (HarperCollins, 2001)

Robin's Room by Margaret Wise Brown (Hyperion Press, 2002)

Suggested Activities with New and Existing Materials:

Students can…

- build models of their bedrooms. Encourage students to refer to the books in the center for construction and extension ideas.

- build model tree houses using the books in the center as reference.

- represent their structures on graph paper or blank paper. Post representations in the center.

SCIENCE CENTER

New Materials:

- **Bathroom Scale**
- **Yardstick or Tape Measure**
- **Stethoscope**
- **Jump Rope**
- **Timer**
- **Mirror**
- **Soap**
- **Window Cleaner**
- **Towels**
- **Poster Size Paper**
- **Markers**

Suggested Activities with New and Existing Materials:

Students can…

- make personal health observations. First, students will measure themselves using the yardstick or tape measure attached to the wall. Next, they listen to their heartbeats while they are sitting still. (Encourage students to count their heartbeats for 10 seconds.) Then, students listen to their heartbeats after jumping rope. (Encourage students to count their heartbeats for 10 seconds.) Finally, students record all of the results. They should share the results with the "doctor" when they go see him or her in the Community Center.

- perform a hand-washing experiment. First, they press their thumbprints on the mirror. Then, students wash their hands, clean the mirror, and press their thumbprints again. (The second print should not show up if all of the oils and germs were washed away.) Students should make posters sharing what they learned about washing their hands.

New Materials:

- **Books**

  Anno's Counting Book by Mitsumasa Anno (HarperTrophy, 1997)

  I Spy Two Eyes: Numbers in Art by Lucy Micklethwait (Mulberry Books, 1998)

- **Hand and Feet Shapes of Various Colors**
- **Magazines**
- **4.25" x 5.5" (108 mm x 139.5 mm) Pieces of Paper—"Photo" Paper**
- **Scissors**
- **Glue**
- **Data for Collection and Graphing—Students' Favorite Foods**
- **Paper Clips as Uniform Units of Measure**
- **Various Objects to Measure in Units of Paper Clips**
- **Jar Filled with Individually Wrapped Candy**

  Chocolates, peppermints, etc.

- **Box for Guesses**

Suggested Activities with New and Existing Materials:

Students can…

- make patterns using the hands and feet shapes. Have students record their patterns.
- sort and classify pictures of people found in magazines. Students should glue individual pictures on photo paper and leave in the center for other students to use.
- interview other students in the center to determine their favorite foods. Students should make graphs of favorite foods.
- measure their hands and feet in units of paper clips. Students should record their measurements.
- measure and record paper clip measurements of various objects.
- estimate the number of candy pieces in the jar. Each student should write his name and estimate on a piece of paper and place it in the box for guesses. When the candy is counted at the end of the unit, the class can see whose estimate came the closest.

New Materials:

- **Books**

  When the Root Children Wake Up by Audrey Wood (Scholastic, Inc., 2002)

  Ed Emberley's Drawing Book of Faces by Ed Emberley (Little, Brown and Company, 1992)

  Looking at Faces in Art by Joy Richardson (Gareth Stevens, 2000)

  Willy's Pictures by Anthony Browne (Candlewick Press, 2000)

- **Apples**
- **Cutting Tools**

  Plastic knives, plastic spoons, and toothpicks for carving apples

- **Mirrors**

Suggested Activities with New and Existing Materials:

Students can…

- construct self-portraits from the recyclable materials.
- paint and/or draw self-portraits.
- trace (outline) a classmate on butcher paper.
- carve apples to look like themselves. Leave the apples in the center to dry.

Friends

Theme Materials & Activities

Themes may last for two to four weeks. You may choose to have some theme centers, as well as some month-by-month centers.

| Reading | Writing | Home Living | Community | Blocks | Science | Math | Art |

READING CENTER

New Materials:

- **Books**

  Best Friends by Steven Kellogg (Puffin Books, 1992)

  Best Friends for Frances by Russell Hoban (HarperTrophy, 1976)

  The Berenstain Bears and the Trouble with Friends by Stan and Jan Berenstain (Random House, 1987)

  Don't Need Friends by Carolyn Crimi (Dragonfly, 2001)

  Friends by Helme Heine (Aladdin Library, 1997)

  George and Martha: The Complete Stories of Two Best Friends by James Marshall (Houghton Mifflin, 1997)

  How to Lose All Your Friends by Nancy Carlson (Puffin Books, 1997)

  We Are Best Friends by Aliki (William Morrow, 1987)

  Yo! Yes? by Chris Raschka (Orchard Books, 1998)

- **Purchased Tapes/CDs**

  Arthur Writes a Story by Marc Brown (Little Brown Audio, 1999)

- **Teacher-Made Tapes**

- **Any Friends Story or Book Read Aloud**

  Taped while being read

- **Sentence Strips for Interactive Chart**

  "Friends" (See page 27 for more information on interactive charts.)

- **"High Five" Wand for Reading the Room**

  A hand shape or glove attached to the end of a pointer or yardstick

- **Predictable Chart**

  "Friends" (See page 27 for more information on interactive charts.)

  - Chart with sentences
  - Cards for sentence building
  - Class book

- **Hugging Bears or Any Matched Pair of Stuffed Toy Animals for Reading Buddies**

- **Chairs, Pillows, or Beanbags for the Special Reading Place**

  Arrange two chairs, pillows, or beanbags so friends are able to sit together to read.

Suggested Activities with New and Existing Materials:

Students can…

- read the books in the center to themselves or to the reading buddies, with emphasis on friends books.

- listen to the stories on tape, with emphasis on friends stories.

- complete and read the interactive charts and predictable charts created during the Friends unit.

- read the room with the "High Five" wand. This activity can be done individually or in pairs.

- read in the Special Reading Place.

WRITING CENTER

New Materials:

- **Books**

    Arthur Writes a Story by Marc Brown (Little, Brown and Company, 1996)

- **Friends Picture Dictionary Chart**

    This is a chart with familiar "Friends" words and pictures such as friends, like, share, play, toys, swing, swim, etc.

- **Friends Shape Books**

    You will find the friends shape book cover on page 139. You will need to cut blank paper to match. Each book should have 4-5 blank pages.

- **Shape Stamps—Children**
- **Clipboard**

Suggested Activities with New and Existing Materials:

Students can…

- write a retelling of a friends story you have read aloud previously or a story they already know. Completed stories may be placed in the Reading Center.
- make a friends picture dictionary.
- write notes to friends. Determine how you want notes delivered so other center activities are not disturbed.
- write the room.

HOME LIVING CENTER

New Materials:
- **Teacups**
- **Saucers**
- **Tablecloths**
- **Napkins**
- **Small Plates**
- **Magazines, Catalogs, Newspaper Ads for Seasonal Objects and Activities**
- **Calendar**
- **Fancy Paper for Invitations**
- **Colorful Markers**
- **Seasonal Clothing and Accessories**

Suggested Activities with New and Existing Materials:

Students can…

- have a tea party with friends.
- plan a seasonal party with friends.
- make invitations for the tea and seasonal parties.
- plan an outing with friends using ideas from magazines, catalogs, newspaper ads.

COMMUNITY CENTER

Game Room

New Materials:
- **Playing Cards**
- **Checkers**
- **Board Games**
- **Puzzle**
- **Pencils**
- **Notepads**

Suggested Activities with New and Existing Materials:

Students can…

- play games with friends. They can use the pencils and notepads to keep score and assess their progress when applicable.

New materials:

- **Books**

    The Clubhouse by Anastasia Suen (Puffin, 2003)

- **Small Toy People**

Suggested Activities with New and Existing Materials:

Students can...

- build models of special places (clubhouses) for themselves and their friends. Encourage students to refer to the books in the center for construction and extension ideas.

- represent their structures on graph paper or blank paper. Post representations in the center.

New Materials:

- **Animals—Mammals**

    Introduce two small mammals (for example, hamsters, gerbils, or mice) to the center. If possible they should be different colors or sizes so students can easily tell them apart. The mammals should remain in the center for the rest of the school year.

    - 10-20 gallon aquarium with mesh lid or hamster/gerbil cage
    - Animal Bedding (pine shavings, recycled paper bedding, cedar shavings, etc.)
    - Toilet paper or paper towel tubes
    - Food for the mammals
    - Toys for the mammals

- **Leaves**
- **Light Table**

    Directions for making a light table can be found at *http://www.spec-tru.com/build_a_light_table.htm.*

Suggested Activities with New and Existing Materials:

Students can...

- observe the new mammals and ask questions, such as:

    How do the mammals interact with each other? Do they act like friends? Is there one place the animals like to spend most of their time? Does each animal have its own special place? How do they eat their food? How do the animals spend most of their time?

- make suggestions for naming the animals. A vote can be taken to select names.

- write and post directions for taking care of the new animals.

- fold or cut a leaf down the middle, make observations, and ask questions, such as:

    Is the leaf the same on both sides? Does it matter which way you fold the leaf?

- observe leaves with the light table, taking particular note of the veins. Leaf observations should be carefully recorded and posted in the center.

New Materials:

- **Book**

  The Water Hole by Graeme Base (Abrams Books for Young Readers, 2001)

- **Children Shapes in Various Colors and Sizes**
- **School Pictures**
- **Graph Paper**
- **Measuring Tape or Yardstick**
- **Jar Filled with "Kid" Counters**

  Counters shaped like children

- **Box for Guesses**

Suggested Activities with New and Existing Materials:

Students can…

- make more complex patterns with a friend. They can use any materials in the center to make their patterns. Have students record their patterns
- sort and classify school pictures by gender, hair color, eye color, etc.
- interview other students in the center for their favorite things to do with a friend. Each student should make a "Favorite Friend Activity" graph.
- measure and record the measurements of a friend.
- estimate the number of "kids" in the jar. Each student should write his name and estimate on a piece of paper and place it in the box for guesses. When the "kids" are counted at the end of the unit, the class can see whose estimate came the closest.
- make lists of their friends and graph school friends versus outside of school friends.

New Materials:

- **Books**

  When the Root Children Wake Up by Audrey Wood (Scholastic, Inc., 2002)

  How Artists See People by Colleen Carroll (Abbeville Press, Inc., 1996)

  Figuring Figures by Brigitte Baumbusch (House of Stratus, 2002)

Suggested Activities with New and Existing Materials:

Students can…

- make portraits of their best friends from recyclable materials.
- paint and/or draw pictures of themselves with their best friends.
- trace outlines on butcher paper of their best friends in the class.

Theme Materials & Activities

Themes may last for two to four weeks. You may choose to have some theme centers, as well as some month-by-month centers.

Reading | Writing | Home Living | Community | Blocks | Science | Math | Art

READING CENTER

New materials:

• **Books**

And to Think That We Thought That We'd Never Be Friends by Mary Ann Hoberman (Dragonfly, 2003)

Families by Ann Morris (HarperCollins, 2000)

Family by Isabell Monk (Lerner Publications Company, 2001)

Goldilocks and the Three Bears by Jan Brett (Puffin Books, 1996)

Grandfather And I by Helen Buckley (Harpercollins Juvenile Books, 2000)

Guess How Much I Love You? by Sam McBratney (Candlewick Press, 1995)

I Love You, Little One by Nancy Tafuri (Cartwheel Books, 2000)

Just Like Dad by Gina and Mercer Mayer (Golden Books Publishing Company, Inc., 1998)

Just Me and My Little Brother by Mercer Mayer (Golden Books Publishing Company, Inc., 1998)

Just Me and My Mom by Mercer Mayer (Golden Books Publishing Company, Inc., 2001)

My Dad Is Awesome by Nick Butterworth (Candlewick Press, 1992)

My Working Mom by Peter Glassman (HarperTrophy, 1994)

The New Baby by Mercer Mayer (Golden Books Publishing Company, Inc., 2001)

Olivia by Ian Falconer (Atheneum, 2000)

On Mother's Lap by Ann Herbert Scott (Clarion Books, 1992)

The Relatives Came by Cynthia Rylant (Pearson Learning, 1993)

This Is My Family by Gina and Mercer Mayer (Golden Books Publishing Company, Inc., 1999)

William's Doll by Charlotte Zolotow (HarperTrophy, 1985)

• **Purchased Tapes/CDs**

On Mother's Lap by Ann Herbert Scott (Clarion Books, 1994)

• **Teacher-Made Tapes**

Any family story or book you read aloud (taped while being read)

• **Sentence Strips for Interactive Charts**

"My Family," "Restaurants" (See page 27 for more information on interactive charts.)

• **Predictable Charts**

"The Relatives Came," "Family," "If I Went to a Restaurant . . ." (See page 27 for more information on predictable charts.)

- Chart with sentences
- Cards for sentence building
- Class book

• **House Wand for Reading the Room**

A small house shape attached to the end of a pointer or yardstick

• **Stuffed Toy Version of "The Three Bears" for Reading Buddies**

Any "family" set of toy stuffed animals

• **Three Chairs (Small, Medium, Large) for the Special Reading Place**

Arrange the three chairs to represent the three bears' chairs and decorate accordingly.

• **Environmental Print—Restaurants**

Cups, boxes, and bags with logos and restaurant names

• **Letter Cards to Spell Restaurant Names**

Suggested Activities with New and Existing Materials:

Students can…

- read the books in the center to themselves or to the reading buddies, with emphasis on the family books.
- listen to the stories on tape, with emphasis on the family stories.
- complete and read the interactive charts and predictable charts made during the family unit.
- read the room with the house wand. This activity can be done individually or in pairs.
- read in the Special Reading Place.
- use letter cards to make words found on the environmental print board.

WRITING CENTER

New Materials:

- **Books**

  Aunt Isabel Tells a Good One by Kate Duke (Puffin Books, 1994)

- **Family Picture Dictionary Chart**

  This is a chart with familiar family words and pictures, such as mom, dad, brother, sister, house, love, family, etc.

- **Shape Books—Faces of Adult and Child, The Three Bears**

  You can make the outline of the shape or you can purchase large shaped notepads from your local school supply store. You will find the shape of an adult's and child's face on page 140. Once you determine what shape you will use, cut blank paper to match. Each book should have 4-5 blank pages.

- **Shape Stamps—Mom, Dad, Children, Grandparents**

- **Clipboard**

Suggested Activities with New and Existing Materials:

Students can…

- write a retelling of a family story you have read aloud previously or a story they already know. Completed stories may be placed in the Reading Center.
- make a family picture dictionary.
- write a memoir of a special family event. Encourage students to tell where they were and what important things happened.
- write the room.

HOME LIVING CENTER

New Materials:

- **Magazines, Catalogs, and Newspaper Ads with Baby Supplies**
- **Baby**
- **Crib**
- **Clothing**
- **Diapers**
- **Books for Baby**
- **Songbooks with Lullabies**

Suggested Activities with New and Existing Materials:

Students can…

- pretend there is a new baby in the family. They will need to set up a baby's room. They should look for ads for needed items, make shopping lists, and get things ready.

Restaurant

New Materials:

- **Table**
- **Chair**
- **Tablecloth**
- **Menus**
- **Plates**
- **Napkins**
- **Silverware**
- **Glasses**
- **Food**

Suggested Activities with New and Existing Materials:

Students can…

- work in and visit the restaurant. Restaurateurs should make menus of what is to be served each day, set the tables, and serve food to the guests.

BLOCKS CENTER

New Materials:

- **Books**

    Building a House by Byron Barton (William Morrow, 1981)

    Bear at Home by Stella Blackstone (Barefoot Books, 2001)

    Houses and Homes by Ann Morris (HarperTrophy, 1995)

    My House by Lisa Desimini (Owlet, 1997)

- **Small Toy People**

Suggested Activities with New and Existing Materials:

Students can…

- build models of their houses or apartments. Encourage students to refer to the books in the center for construction and extension ideas.
- represent their structures on graph paper or blank paper. Post representations in the center.

SCIENCE CENTER

New Materials:

- **Beet Juice**

    Wash and slice a fresh beet. Place about four slices of the beet into a sauce pan containing 1 cup of water. Heat until boiling and continue heating for about 5 minutes. Remove the beet slices and allow the red liquid to cool. Store in the refrigerator until it is used.

- **Vinegar**
- **Red Cabbage Juice**

    Chop up a head of red cabbage, place it in a sauce pan, cover with water, and simmer until the water becomes dark purple. Let the cabbage and water

cool, discard the cabbage, and store the remaining liquid in the refrigerator until it is used.

- **Water**
- **Baking Soda**
- **Flour**
- **Corn Starch**
- **Sugar**
- **Salt**
- **Talcum Powder**
- **Any Other White Powder**
- **Small Plastic Spoon**

- **Eye Droppers or Larger Medicine Droppers**
- **Toothpicks (optional)**
- **Muffin Tins**
- **Kitchen Chemistry Log**
- **Aprons or Smocks**

Suggested Activities with New and Existing Materials:

Students can…

- test each powder with one of the solutions. Students should wear aprons or smocks over their clothing for this activity as some of the solutions will stain clothing.

- Students place a small spoonful of powder in the bottom of each section in the muffin tin. They begin by testing all powders with one

of the solutions and recording what happened. Students can further mix the powder and solution with the toothpick.

- Muffin tins should be rinsed and dried before testing the next solution.

- Students should continue to experiment with various combinations, making sure they record their findings.

Note: Students may need some supervision with this activity. Be sure students do not taste test ANY of the solutions or powders. Beet juice turns red when in contact with acids (vinegar) and turns blue when in contact with alkalines (baking soda). Red cabbage juice turns red or pink when in contact with acids (vinegar) and turns green when in contact with alkalines (baking soda). All samples must be discarded after testing.

MATH CENTER

New Materials:

- **Books**

  Feast for Ten by Cathryn Falwell (Clarion Books, 1995)

  Five Little Monkeys Jumping on the Bed by Eileen Christelow (Scott Foresman, 1989)

- **People Shapes in Various Sizes and Colors**
- **Bears of Any Kind**

  Counters, stickers, pictures, etc.

- **Data for Collection and Graphing–Students' Favorite Family Members**
- **Measuring Spoons and Measuring Cups**
- **Pitchers of Water**
- **Large Tub to Hold Water**
- **Jar Filled with Heart or Red Cinammon Imperials Candy**
- **Box for Guesses**

Suggested Activities with New and Existing Materials:

Students can…

- make patterns with the people shapes. Have students record their patterns

- sort and classify bears (counters, stickers, pictures, etc.)

- determine how many tablespoons and teaspoons are in 1/4 cup, 1/2 cup, and 1 cup. They should record the equivalent measures.

- interview the other students in the center to determine their favorite family members. Students should make graphs of their favorite family members.

- estimate the number of heart candy pieces (or red cinammon imperials) in the jar. Each student should write his name and estimate on a piece of paper and place it in the box for guesses. When the heart candy pieces (or red cinammon imperials) are counted at the end of the unit, the class can see whose estimate came the closest.

New Materials:

• **Books**

Ed Emberley's Drawing Book of Faces by Ed Emberley (Little, Brown and Company, 1992)

Families by Ann Morris (HarperCollins, 2000)

How Artists See Families by Colleen Carroll (Abbeville Press, Inc., 2000)

Looking at Faces in Art by Joy Richardson (Gareth Stevens, 2000)

Suggested Activities with New and Existing Materials:

Students can…

• make family portraits from recyclable materials.

• paint and/or draw family portraits. Encourage students to frame their work with construction paper.

Theme Materials & Activities

Themes may last for two to four weeks. You may choose to have some theme centers, as well as some month-by-month centers.

| Reading | Writing | Home Living | Community | Blocks | Science | Math | Art |

READING CENTER

New Materials:

- **Books**

  Annabelle Swift, Kindergartner by Amy Schwartz (Orchard Books, 1991)

  Bartholomew and the Oobleck by Dr. Seuss (Random House, 1970)

  First Day, Hooray! by Nancy Poydar (Holiday House, 2000)

  First Day Jitters by Julie Danneberg (Charlesbridge Publishing, 2000)

  Froggy Goes to School by Jonathan London (Puffin Books, 1998)

  The Kissing Hand by Audrey Penn (Child Welfare League of America, 1993)

  Little Miss Spider at Sunnypatch School by David Kirk (Scholastic, Inc., 2000)

  Look Out Kindergarten Here I Come! by Nancy Carlson (Puffin Books, 1999)

  Miss Bindergarten Gets Ready for Kindergarten by Joseph Slate (Puffin Books, 2001)

  Miss Nelson Is Missing! by Harry Allard (Houghton Mifflin, 1985)

  My Teacher Sleeps in School by Leatie Weiss (Puffin Books, 1985)

  School by Emily McCully (Harpercollins Juvenile Books, 1990)

  Tiptoe into Kindergarten by Jacqueline Rogers (Cartwheel Books, 2003)

  Will I Have a Friend? by Miriam Cohen (Aladdin Library, 1989)

- **Purchased Tapes/CDs**

  Miss Nelson Is Missing! by Harry Allard (Houghton Mifflin, 1993)

- **Teacher-Made Tapes**

  Any story or book you read aloud (taped while being read)

- **Sentence Strips for Interactive Chart**

  "Rainbows (in My Classroom)" (See page 27 for more information on interactive charts.)

- **Predictable Charts**

  "At the School Assembly," "At the Library," "School" (See page 27 for more information on predictable charts.)
  - Charts with sentences
  - Cards for sentence building
  - Class books

- **Bus Wand for Reading the Room**

  A bus shape attached to the end of a pointer or yardstick

- **Stuffed Toy Storybook Characters for Reading Buddies**

- **"Teacher's" Desk for Special Reading Place**

  Set up a "teacher's" desk in the center and use it for the Special Reading Place

Suggested Activities with New and Existing Materials:

Students can...

- read the books in the center to themselves or to the reading buddies, with emphasis on the school books.

- listen to the stories on tape, with emphasis on the school stories.

- complete and read the interactive chart and predictable charts created during the school unit.

- read the room with the bus wand. This activity can be done individually or in pairs.

- read in the Special Reading Place.

WRITING CENTER

New Materials:

- **Book**

    From Pictures to Words: A Book About Making a Book by Janet Stevens (Holiday House, 1999)

- **School Picture Dictionary Chart**

    This is a chart with familiar school words and pictures such as teacher, student, read, write, recess, lunch, etc.

- **School Shape Books—School and Bus**

    You can make the outline of the shape or you can purchase large shaped notepads from your local school supply store. Once you determine what shape you will use, cut blank paper to match. Each book should have 4-5 blank pages.

- **Shape Stamps—School-Related Items**

    Desks, books, pencils, etc.

- **Clipboard**

Suggested activities with New and Existing Materials:

Students can…

- write a retelling of a school story you have read aloud previously or a story students already know. Completed stories may be placed in the Reading Center.

- make a school picture dictionary.

- write about their favorite school-related activity, person, subject, etc.

- write the room.

HOME LIVING CENTER

New materials:

- **Back-to-School Magazines, Catalogs, and Newspaper Ads**
- **"New" School Clothes**
- **"Teacher" Clothes**

Suggested Activities with New and Existing Materials:

Students can…

- get ready for school. They can make lists of school supplies they need, new clothes they want, lunch box items, etc.

- get ready for their first day at school as a "teacher." They can make lists of supplies they need, new clothes they want, students in their classes, etc.

COMMUNITY CENTER

School

New materials:

- **Desks**
- **Chalkboard**
- **School Supplies**
- **Backpacks**
- **Lunch Boxes**

- **Books**
- **Manipulatives**
- **Letters**
- **Paper**
- **Pencils**

Suggested Activities with New and Existing Materials:

Students can...

- go to school with their friends. One student can be the teacher while others participate as students.

BLOCKS CENTER

New Materials:

- **Books**

    Froggy Goes to School by Jonathan London (Puffin Books, 1998)

    Miss Bindergarten Gets Ready for Kindergarten by Joseph Slate (Puffin Books, 2001)

    My Teacher Sleeps in School by Leatie Weiss (Puffin Books, 1985)

Suggested Activities with New and Existing Materials:

Students can...

- build models of their school. Encourage students to refer to the books in the center for construction and extension ideas.

SCIENCE CENTER

New Materials:

- **Book**

    Bartholomew and the Oobleck by Dr. Seuss (Random House, 1970)

- **Boxes of Corn Starch**
- **Water**
- **Bowl**
- **Green Food Coloring (optional)**
- **Sand**
- **Cooking Oil**
- **Resealable Plastic Bags**
- **Several Small Containers of Water**

Suggested Activities with New and Existing Materials:

Students can...

- make Oobleck after hearing the Dr. Seuss story. Students should measure and mix (using their fingers) 1 box of cornstarch with 14 ounces (420 ml) of water. Store and/or send home in plastic bags or containers with lids. Students can describe how Oobleck is like water and how it is like dough.

Note: Students should need minimal supervision with this activity. Although mixing the powder and liquid might be a bit messy, there is nothing that can harm students or damage other materials.

- mix a cup of sand with a tablespoon of cooking oil in a resealable plastic bag. After students mix the sand and oil by gently squeezing the bag they can see how it is different from sand without oil.

- Have students drop a spoonful of regular sand in one container of water. Then, have them drop a spoonful of oily sand in another container of water. What happened when the regular sand went into the water? What happened when the oily sand went into the water?

- Have students scoop the regular sand out of the water. Then, have them scoop the oily sand out of the water. How are they the same? How are they different?

Note: Students should need minimal supervision with this activity. Although the sand and oil mixture might be a bit messy, there is nothing that can harm students or damage other materials.

New Materials:

- **Books**

  Ten, Nine, Eight by Molly Garret Bang (HarperTrophy, 1991)

- **Shapes of Children in Various Sizes and Colors**
- **Pencils of Various Sizes and Colors**
- **Data for Collection and Graphing—Students' Favorite School Activities**
- **Pencil Top Erasers as Units of Measure**
- **Jar Filled with Pencil Top Erasers**
- **Box for Guesses**

Suggested Activities with New and Existing Materials:

Students can...

- make patterns with shapes of children. Have students record their patterns.
- sort and classify pencils by size and color.
- interview other students in the center about their favorite school activities. Students should make favorite school activity graphs.
- measure objects in the math center using pencil top erasers as units of measure. Students should record measurements.
- estimate the number of pencil top erasers in the jar. Each student should write her name and estimate on a piece of paper and place it in the box for guesses. When the erasers are counted at the end of the unit, the class can see whose estimate came the closest.

New Materials:

- **Books**

  Ed Emberley's Drawing Book of Faces by Ed Emberley (Little, Brown and Company, 1992)

  Looking at Faces in Art by Joy Richardson (Gareth Stevens, 2000)

- **Old School or Class Yearbooks**
- **Blank "Yearbooks"**
- **Magazines**

Suggested Activities with New and Existing Materials:

Students can...

- use recyclables to make and/or decorate school items such as pencil holders, book boxes (made from cereal boxes), or desk nameplates.

- make class yearbooks, including all of their classmates and the things they have done this year. Students should cut out pictures from magazines and draw themselves and their friends in the photos. They should glue the pictures in their "yearbooks."

Theme Materials & Activities

Themes may last for two to four weeks. You may choose to have some theme centers, as well as some month-by-month centers.

| Reading | Writing | Home Living | Community | Blocks | Science | Math | Art |

READING CENTER

New Materials:

- **Books**

    The Carrot Seed by Ruth Krauss (HarperTrophy, 1989)

    Eating the Alphabet: Fruits and Vegetables from A to Z by Lois Ehlert (Voyager Books, 1993)

    Flower Garden by Eve Bunting (Voyager Books, 2000)

    From Seed to Plant by Gail Gibbons (Holiday House, 1993)

    Growing Vegetable Soup by Lois Ehlert (Voyager Books, 1990)

    Jack's Garden by Henry Cole (Scott Foresman, 1995)

    Johnny Appleseed by Steven Kellogg (Harpercollins Juvenile Books, 1996)

    The Reason for a Flower by Ruth Heller (Puffin Books, 1999)

    The Rose in My Garden by Arnold Lobel (HarperTrophy, 1993)

    The Tiny Seed by Eric Carle (Aladdin Library, 2001)

    Tops & Bottoms by Janet Stevens (Harcourt, 1995)

    A Tree Is Nice by Janice May Udry (HarperTrophy, 1987)

    Sky Tree: Seeing Science Through Art by Thomas Locker (HarperTrophy, 2001)

- **Purchased Tapes/CDs**

    The Reason for a Flower by Ruth Heller (Spoken Arts, 1999)

- **Teacher-Made Tapes**

    Any story or book you read aloud (recorded while being read)

- **Sentence Strips for Interactive Chart**

    "Plants" (See page 27 for more information on interactive charts.)

- **Predictable Charts**

    "Eating the Alphabet," "Johnny Appleseed," "Plants," "If I Had a Garden" (See page 27 for more information on interactive charts.)
    - Charts with sentences
    - Cards for sentence building
    - Class books

- **Flower Wand for Reading the Room**

    A flower attached to the end of a pointer or yardstick

- **Stuffed Toy Flowers, Vegetables, or Any Other Stuffed Toy Plant or Plant Pillows for Reading Buddies**

- **A Flower Garden for the Special Reading Place**

    Create a garden using paper flowers and vines to surround one part of the center.

Suggested Activities with New and Existing Materials:

Students can...

- read the books in the center to themselves or to the reading buddies, with emphasis on the plant books.

- listen to the new books on tape, with emphasis on the plant stories.

- complete and read the interactive charts and predictable charts made during the Plants unit.

- read the room with the flower wand. This activity can be done individually or in pairs.

- read in the Special Reading Place.

New Materials:

• **Books**

How a Book Is Made by Aliki (HarperTrophy, 1988)

• **Plants Picture Dictionary Chart**

This is a chart with familiar plant words and pictures such as flower, vegetables, leaves, petals, water, seed, dirt, etc.

• **Plants Shape Books—Flowers, Flowerpot, Tree**

You will find the shape of a tree on page 141. You can make the outline of the other shapes or you can purchase large shaped notepads from your local school supply store. Once you determine what shape you will use, cut blank paper to match. Each book should have 4-5 blank pages.

• **Shape Stamps—Plants, Flowers, Trees, Pots**
• **Clipboard**

Suggested Activities with New and Existing Materials:

Students can…

• write a retelling of a plant story you have read aloud previously or a story they already know. Completed stories may be placed in the Reading Center.

• make a plant picture dictionary.

• write directions for planting a seed or taking care of a plant. The directions may be posted in the Science and Home Living Centers.

• write the room.

New Materials:

• **Spring and Gardening Magazines, Catalogs, and Newspaper Ads**
• **Gardening Clothes**
• **Gloves**
• **Knee Pads**
• **Hats**

Suggested Activities with New and Existing Materials:

Students can…

• prepare to do some gardening. They can use the magazines, catalogs, and newspaper ads to make lists of what they will need for their gardens.

• cut out pictures, glue on index size pieces of paper, and write the name of the supplies to make coupons.

Garden Center

New Materials:

• **Pots**
• **Shovels**
• **Buckets**
• **Plastic/Cloth Flowers**

Suggested Activities with New and Existing Materials:

Students can…

• create a "garden center." Mark off a section of the community center with masking tape. Create rows with the tape for plants to be planted. There should be a place for customers to purchase and return plants.

• make labels and signs for the "garden center."

BLOCKS CENTER

New Materials:

- **Books**

  Flower Garden by Eve Bunting (Voyager Books, 2000)

  Jack's Garden by Henry Cole (Scott Foresman, 1995)

Suggested Activities with New and Existing Materials:

Students can…

- build models of gardens or garden centers. Encourage students to refer to the books in the center for construction and extension ideas.

- represent their structures on graph paper or blank paper. Post representations in the center.

SCIENCE CENTER

New materials:

- **Apples—Variety of Sizes and Colors**
- **Balance Scale and Weights**
- **Seeds**

  Any type of seed will work well. Check with the local garden center for a plant that will grow well in your area when planted outside in the spring.

- **Cups—Plastic or Foam**
- **Dirt/Potting Soil**
- **Plastic Tablecloth**
- **Plastic Spoons**
- **Watering Can**
- **Craft Sticks**
- **Seed Packet Sized Pieces of Paper**
- **Empty Seed Packets (as Examples)**
- **Markers**
- **Glue**

Suggested Activities with New and Existing Materials:

Students can…

- weigh and sort the apples.

- decorate cups for their new plants. They may use the markers or any other materials available.

- plant the seeds in their newly decorated cups. Encourage students to work on the plastic tablecloth and keep the dirt and watering can in that space.

Note: Students should need minimal supervision with this activity. Although the dirt might be a bit messy, there is nothing that can harm students or damage other materials.

- make name cards for their plants. These name cards should tell who planted the seed, what kind of seed it is, and how to care for the plant. Students should create "seed packets" with the necessary information, using the seed packet sized pieces of paper. These can be glued to craft sticks and placed in the cups.

- continue to observe and care for the plants and animals in the center.

New Materials:

- **Books**

  Ten Little Ladybugs by Melanie Gerth (Piggy Toes Press, 2001)

  Ten Red Apples by Pat Hutchins (Greenwillow Books, 2000)

- **Patterns—Plant and Flower Shapes of Various Sizes and Colors**
- **Leaves and Seeds of Various Sizes and Shapes**
- **Data for Collection and Graphing—Students' Favorite Flowers**
- **Silk and Plastic Flowers with Stems**
- **Unsharpened Pencils as Units of Measure**
- **Jar Filled with Seeds**
- **Box for Guesses**

Suggested Activities with New and Existing Materials:

Students can…

- make patterns with shapes of plants and flowers. Have students record their patterns.
- sort and classify the leaves and seeds by size, color, and shape.
- interview the other students in the center about their favorite flowers. Students should make favorite flower graphs.
- measure the silk and plastic flowers using the unsharpened pencils as units of measure. Students should record measurements.
- estimate the number of seeds in the jar. Each student should write his name and estimate on a piece of paper and place it in the box for guesses. When the seeds are counted at the end of the unit, the class can see whose estimate came the closest.

New Materials:

- **Books**

  Flower Garden by Eve Bunting (Voyager Books, 2000)

  Claude Monet: Sunshine and Waterlilies by True Kelley (Grossett & Dunlap, 2001)

- **Still Life Picture of Flowers**
- **Water Colors**
- **Apples from Science Center**

  Or substitute potatoes

- **Stamp Pads or Tempera Paint in Small Containers**

Suggested Activities with New and Existing Materials:

Students can…

- make flowers from recyclable materials.
- draw and paint their own versions of the flower still life.
- make apple (or potato) stamps.

Theme Materials & Activities

Themes may last for two to four weeks. You may choose to have some theme centers, as well as some month-by-month centers.

| Reading | Writing | Home Living | Community | Blocks | Science | Math | Art |

READING CENTER

New Materials:

- **Books**

Birds

All About Owls by Jim Arnosky (Scholastic, Inc., 1999)

Birds by Brian Wildsmith (Oxford Press, 1996)

Birdsong by Audrey Wood (Voyager Books, 2001)

The Chick and the Duckling by Mirra Ginsburg (Aladdin Library, 1988)

Edward the Emu by Sheena Knowles (HarperTrophy, 1998)

The Emperor's Egg by Martin Jenkins (Candlewick Press, 2002)

Feathers for Lunch by Lois Ehlert (Voyager Books, 1996)

Have You Seen My Duckling? by Nancy Tafuri (HarperTrophy, 1991)

What Makes a Bird a Bird? by May Garelick (Mondo Publishing, 1995)

Frogs and Toads

The Big Wide-Mouthed Frog: A Traditional Tale by Ana Larranaga (Candlewick Press, 1999)

Climbing Tree Frogs by Ruth Berman (Lerner Publications Company, 1998)

Froggy's First Kiss by Jonathan London (Puffin Books, 1999)

The Icky Sticky Frog by Dawn Bentley (Piggy Toes Press, 2001)

Jump, Frog, Jump by Robert Kalan (HarperTrophy, 1989)

Lizards, Frogs, and Polliwogs by Douglas Florian (Harcourt, 2001)

The Mysterious Tadpole by Steven Kellogg (Puffin Books, 1992)

One Frog Too Many by Mercer Mayer (Puffin Books, 1992)

A Salamander's Life by John Himmelman (Children's Book Press, 1998)

General

Mammalabilia by Douglas Florian (Harcourt, 2000)

I Took a Walk by Henry Cole (Greenwillow Books, 1998)

Insects

Alpha Bugs: A Pop-Up Alphabet by David Carter (Little Simon, 1994)

Antics!: An Alphabetical Anthology by Cathi Hepworth (Puffin Books, 1996)

Are You A Snail? by Judy Allen and Tudor Humphries (Kingfisher, 2000)

Backyard Detective: Critters Up Close by Nic Bishop (Scholastic, Inc., 2002)

Bugs! Bugs! Bugs! by Bob Barner (Chronicle Books, 1999)

The Grouchy Ladybug by Eric Carle (HarperTrophy, 1996)

Hey Little Ant by Phillip and Hannah Hoose (Tricycle Press, 1998)

Insectlopedia: Poems and Paintings by Douglas Florian (Voyager Books, 2002)

Ladybug, Ladybug by Ruth Brown (Puffin Books, 1992)

Miss Spider's Tea Party by David Kirk (Scholastic, Inc., 1994)

A Pill Bug's Life by John Himmelman (Children's Book Press, 2000)

The Very Quiet Cricket by Eric Carle (Philomel Books, 1990)

Pets

Can I Keep Him? by Steven Kellogg (Puffin Books, 1992)

Cats, Cats, Cats! by Leslea Newman (Simon & Schuster, Inc., 2001)

Clifford, the Big Red Dog by Norman Bridwell (Scholastic, Inc., 1985)

Good Dog, Carl by Alexandra Day (Aladdin Library, 1996)

Hamsters and Gerbils by Ann Larkin Hansen (Checkerboard Library, 1997)

If You Give a Mouse a Cookie by Laura Joffe Numeroff (HarperTrophy, 1997)

I'll Always Love You by Hans Wilhelm (Crown Publishing Group, 1989)

Mrs. McTats and Her Houseful of Cats by Alyssa Satin Capucilli (Margaret K. McElderry Books, 2001)

My Dog Rosie by Isabelle Harper (Scholastic, Inc., 1999)

The Perfect Pet by Carol Chataway (Kids Can Press, 2002)

A Pup Just For Me/A Boy Just For Me by Dorothea P. Seeber (Puffin Books, 2002)

Rosie: A Visiting Dog's Story by Stephanie Calmenson (Houghton Mifflin, 1998)

Sally Goes to the Beach by Stephen Huneck (Harry N. Abrams, Inc., 2000)

Whistle for Willie by Ezra Jack Keats (Puffin Books, 1977)

- **Purchased Tapes/CDs**

  Clifford, the Big Red Dog by Norman Bridwell (Scholastic Audio Cassette, 1988)

  If You Give a Mouse a Cookie by Laura Joffe Numeroff (HarperFestival, 1994)

- **Teacher-Made Tapes**
  Any story or book you read aloud (recorded while being read)

- **Sentence Strips for Interactive Charts**
  "Insects," "Birds," "Frogs and Toads," "Pets" (See page 27 for more information on interactive charts.)

- **Predictable Charts**
  "Pets," "If I Had a Pet" (See page 27 for more information on predictable charts.)
  - Charts with sentences
  - Cards for sentence building
  - Class books

- **Fly Swatter Wand for Reading the Room**
  You may want to cut out an area in the middle to highlight words.

- **Any Stuffed Toy Animal that Matches the Topic for Reading Buddies**
  Insects, birds, frogs and toads, pets, dinosaurs, or farm animals

- **"Dog" Bed for the Special Reading Place**
  Use throw pillows to make a dog bed. Students can lay on the "bed" while they read.

Suggested Activities with New Materials:
Students can…

- read the books in the center to themselves or to the reading buddies, with emphasis on the animal books.

- listen to the stories on tape, with emphasis on the animal stories.

- complete and read the interactive charts and predictable charts made during the Animals unit.

- read the room with the fly swatter wand. This activity can be done individually or in pairs.

- read in the Special Reading Place.

Place posters in centers to provide students with additional support. Animal posters in the Science Center and book posters in the Reading Center encourage students to use these as resources. Don't forget to change the posters as you change your centers monthly or according to a theme.

New Materials:

- **Books:**
  What Do Authors Do? by Eileen Christelow
  (Houghton Mifflin, 1997)

- **Animals Picture Dictionary Chart**
  This is a chart with familiar "animal" words and pictures such as bugs, pets, dog, cat, frog, toad, cricket, grasshopper, etc.

- **Animal Shape Books—Insect, Bird, and Frog**
  You can make the outline of the shape or you can purchase large shaped notepads from your local school supply store. Once you determine what shape you are going to use, you will need to cut blank paper to match. Each book should have 4-5 blank pages.

- **Shape Stamps—Animal Stamps**
  especially bugs, pets, frogs, or toads

- **Clipboard**

Suggested Activities with New and Existing Materials:
Students can...

- write a retelling of an animal story you have read aloud previously or a story they already know. Completed stories may be placed in the Reading Center.

- make an animal picture dictionary.

- write a story about a pet or an animal they know.

- write the room.

HOME LIVING CENTER

New Materials:
- **Pet Magazines, Catalogs, Newspaper Ads**
- **Animal Food and Bowl**
- **Small Animal Bed**
- **Leash**
- **Stuffed Toy Pets**
  For example, cat or dog

Suggested Activities with New and Existing Materials:
Students can...

- set up a home for a new pet. Students can make lists of the supplies they will need to take care of their new pets. They can set up a place in the center for their pets.

HOME LIVING CENTER

Veterinarian's Office

New Materials:
- **Telephone**
- **Message Pad**
- **Appointment Book**
- **Stethoscope**
- **Thermometer**
- **Tongue Depressors**
- **Bandages**
- **Bathroom Scale**

Suggested Activities with New and Existing Materials:
Students can...

- take their new pets to the vet. A receptionist should take appointments. A nurse should weigh and measure the pets. A vet should record how the pet is feeling and write prescriptions. The nurse can "fill" the prescriptions.

New Materials:

- **Books**

  Backyard Detective: Critters Up Close by Nic Bishop (Scholastic, Inc.., 2002)

  Feathers for Lunch by Lois Ehlert (Voyager Books, 1996)

  Hamsters and Gerbils by Ann Larkin Hansen (Checkerboard Library, 1997)

  Jump, Frog, Jump by Robert Kalan (HarperTrophy, 1989)

  What Makes a Bird a Bird? by May Garelick (Mondo Publishing, 1995)

Suggested Activities with New and Existing Materials:

Students can…

- build animals or animal homes with blocks. Encourage students to refer to the books in the center for construction and extension ideas.

- represent their structures on graph paper or blank paper. Post representations in the center.

New Materials:

- **Insects—Rotting Log**

  Find a good-sized rotting log. Put the log in a large plastic container (approximately 58 quart/55 liter depending upon the size of the log) with lid. Add a small amount of soil. The log should be full of insects, and hopefully larvae, for children to observe. The insects will stay in the container as long as the lid is on when not in use. The insects are decomposing (eating) the log. Students should notice that dirt is "growing" in the bottom of the container. The only care for the log is a light misting of water every day. The log should remain in the center as long as insects are found. Insects and larvae can be "hunted" and added in the spring.

- **Insects—Crickets**

  Purchase crickets by the tube from a local bait shop. While you are there notice the other animals that are available. These animals are not only inexpensive, they represent animals that live in the area and what students would be able to find in the their own backyards. Crickets should remain in the center for as long as possible.

  - 10-20 gallon aquarium with mesh lid
  - Toilet paper or paper towel tubes
  - Cedar chips
  - Dog food
  - Apples
  - Shallow water container, cotton pad in bottom

- **Animals—Mudpuppy (Salamander)**

  Purchase a mudpuppy at a local bait shop or pet store. Mudpuppy is the common term for an aquatic animal that looks like a large tadpole with legs and frilly gills. The term mudpuppy, or "water dog," is broadly used for various types of salamanders. The mudpuppy you find may be a mudpuppy, an axolotl, or a larval (tadpole stage) tiger salamander. Mudpuppies and axolotls retain their gills for their entire lives. Larval tiger salamanders will transform, like all larval stage animals, into adult tiger salamanders, losing their gills and tails. In all species, watch for changes in gills and general activity level. These may be indicators of transformation or a need to clean or add water.

  The mudpuppy can live in a small aquarium filled about ¾ full. It likes to hide so arrange rocks in the bottom with areas where they can hide. The mudpuppy is a hearty animal and should remain in the center for the rest of the school year.

  If your mudpuppy is a larval salamander, it may not transform during the school year. If it does, the aquarium needs to also transform. Significantly reduce the amount of water to create an aqua-terrarium. Leave a shallow amount of water (1-2"/ 2.5-5cm) in the bottom with plenty of rocks, soil, or peat. Half of the aqua-terrarium should allow the salamander access to water, the other half to dry land.

It is a good idea to get additional information by searching the Internet or purchasing a book on mudpuppies and salamanders.

- 10-20 gallon aquarium
- Rocks
- Food (brine shrimp, tubifex worm cubes, food sticks, or pellets)

• **Animals—Worms**

Worms can be purchased at a bait shop or on-line. There are two different kinds of worms found in most bait shops. If you can get red wrigglers, they will decompose raw fruits and vegetables. Night crawlers do not decompose; they only dig holes to aerate the soil. Worms should remain in the center for as long as possible.

- Any large container (preferably one that is clear so students can observe worms in the soil)
- Dirt/potting soil
- Raw fruits and vegetables (if using red wrigglers)

• **Animals—Fish**

Fish will need an aquarium, rocks, and appropriate food. Some fish will require oxygenation systems. A Beta makes a good fish. They don't require an oxygenation system and they can live in very small containers. Goldfish may not be the best fish to purchase. They do require oxygenation. Once added, the fish should remain in the center for the rest of the school year.

• **Animals—Mammals**

Introduce two small mammals (for example, hamsters, gerbils, or mice) to the center. If possible they should be different colors or sizes so students can easily tell them apart. The mammal should remain in the center for the rest of the school year.

- 10-20 gallon aquarium with mesh lid or hamster/gerbil cage
- Animal bedding (pine shavings, recycled paper bedding, cedar shavings, etc.)
- Toilet paper or paper towel tubes
- Food for the mammals
- Toys for the mammals

• **Hand Sprayer/Mister**
• **Plastic Spoons**
• **Large Wooden Spoons**
• **Paper Plates**
• **Disposable Ice Cream Sundae Dishes**
• **Magnifying Glasses**

• **Animal Record Logs**

Suggested Activities with New and Existing Materials:

Students can…

- write and post directions for taking care of the different animals.

- observe animals on the rotten log.

  Students should put a scoop of dirt from the log in one of the dishes to see what they can find using the magnifying glass.

  Students should collect insects from the log and place them in the dishes for further observation.

- observe crickets. Count the number of cricket chirps. Count the number of cricket jumps. Count the number of crickets on an object.

- observe the mudpuppy. Encourage students to use the resources in the center as they observe the mudpuppy. Some questions to guide observations: How does the mudpuppy spend most of its time? How does the mudpuppy look like a tadpole? How is it different? Does it remind young scientists of anything else?

- observe the worms.

If you get red wrigglers, students can:

- feed the worms leftovers from lunch (no meat—fruits, vegetables, bread, rice, etc.). See how long it takes to decompose an apple, a banana peel, a raw carrot stick, etc.

- count the number of worms on any piece of fruit or vegetable.

If you get night crawlers, students can:

- take one worm out and measure how long it is.

- see how many worms they can dig up with one spoonful of dirt.

- observe the fish. Does the fish have a particular place in the bowl that it likes to be? Students can use the magnifying glass to see if they can identify any specific details. Details should be recorded in a drawing of the fish.

- observe the new mammals. How do the mammals interact with each other? Do they act like friends? Is there one place the animals like to spend most of their time? Does each animal have its own special place? How do they eat their food? How do the animals spend most of their time?

New Materials:

- **Books**

   Mrs. McTats and Her Houseful of Cats by Alyssa Satin Capucilli (Margaret K. McElderry Books, 2001)

   How Many Bugs in a Box? by David A. Carter (Little Simon, 1988)

- **Shapes of Different Animals**
- **Plastic Bugs**
- **Data for Collecting and Graphing—Students' Favorite Animals**
- **Ruler**
- **Gummy Worms**
- **Jar Filled with Gummy Worms**
- **Box for Guesses**

Suggested Activities with New and Existing Materials:

Students can…

- make patterns with the shapes of animals. Have students record their patterns.
- sort and classify plastic bugs by size, number of legs, color, shape, etc.
- interview the other students in the center to determine their favorite animals. Students should make favorite animal graphs.
- measure a gummy worm with a ruler. Students should record their measurements.
- estimate the number of gummy worms in the jar. Each student should write her estimate on a piece of paper and place it in the box for guesses. When the gummy worms are counted at the end of the unit, the class can see whose estimate came the closest.

New Materials:

- **Books**

   Ed Emberley's Drawing Book of Animals by Ed Emberley (Little, Brown and Company, 1994)

   How Artists See Animals by Colleen Carroll (Abbeville Press, Inc., 1999)

- **Tables for Display**
- **Craft Paper for Backdrops**

Suggested Activities with New and Existing Materials:

Students can…

- make animals from recyclable materials.
- paint and/or draw animals.
- make animals from clay.
- place animals on a mural or tables to create habitats. Students can also use the craft paper to create backdrops for their habitats.

Dinosaurs

Theme Materials & Activities

Themes may last for two to four weeks. You may choose to have some theme centers, as well as some month-by-month centers.

| Reading | Writing | Home Living | Community | Blocks | Science | Math | Art |

READING CENTER

New Materials:

- **Books**

    ABC T-Rex by Bernard Most (Harcourt, 2000)

    Can I Have a Stegosaurus, Mom? Can I? Please!? by Lois Grambling (Troll, 1998)

    Dinosaur Bones by Bob Barner (Chronicle Books, 2001)

    Dinosaur Roar! by Paul and Henrietta Stickland (Puffin Books, 2002)

    Dinosaur Stomp!: A Monster Pop-Up Book by Paul Stickland (Dutton Books, 1996)

    Dinosaurs, Dinosaurs by Byron Barton (Harpercollins Juvenile Books, 1991)

    Saturday Night at the Dinosaur Stomp by Carol Diggery Shields (Candlewick Press, 2002)

    Ten Little Dinosaurs by Pattie Schnetzler (Accord Publishing, Ltd., 1996)

    Ten Terrible Dinosaurs by Paul Stickland (Puffin Books, 2000)

    Whatever Happened to the Dinosaurs? by Bernard Most (Voyager Books, 1987)

- **Teacher-Made Tapes**

    Any story or book you read aloud (recorded while being read)

- **Dinosaur Wand for Reading the Room**

    Dinosaur shape attached to the end of a yardstick or pointer

- **Stuffed Toy Dinosaurs for Reading Buddies**

- **Large Craft Paper Tree for the Special Reading Place**

    Twist brown craft paper to make tree limbs. Cut green paper to make a large canopy of leaves. Make the tree low to the ground so students feel they are reading under the tree.

Suggested Activities with New and Existing Materials:

Students can…

- read the books in the center to themselves or to the reading buddies, with emphasis on the dinosaur books.

- listen to the stories on tape, with emphasis on the dinosaur stories.

- read the room with the dinosaur wand. This activity can be done individually or in pairs.

- read in the Special Reading Place.

WRITING CENTER

New Materials:

- **Books:**

    Dinosaurs, Dinosaurs by Byron Barton (Harpercollins Juvenile Books, 1991)

- **Dinosaur Picture Dictionary Chart**

    This is a chart with familiar dinosaur words and pictures such as dinosaur, brontosaurus, tyrannosaurus rex, extinct, etc.

- **Dinosaur Shape Books**

    You will find a dinosaur shape on page 141. You will need to cut blank paper to match. Each book should have 4-5 blank pages.

- **Shape Stamps—Dinosaurs**
- **Clipboard**

Suggested Activities with New and Existing Materials:

Students can…

- write a retelling of a dinosaur story you have read aloud previously or a story they already know. Completed stories may be placed in the Reading Center.
- make a dinosaur picture dictionary.
- write a story about a dinosaur movie they have seen.
- write the room.

HOME LIVING CENTER

New Materials:

- **Table or Desk**
- **Tablecloth**
- **Place Cards**

    Or blank pieces of paper cut and folded to stand

- **Khaki Clothing**
- **Safari Hats**
- **Netting**

Suggested Activities with New and Existing Materials:

Students can…

- dress to work in the Dinosaur Dig (Community Center, below).
- set up a display to share their findings in the dig. Items should be placed on the display table and properly labeled.

COMMUNITY CENTER

Dinosaur Dig

New Materials:

- **Sand Table or Small Wading Pool**
- **Sand**
- **Shovels**
- **Buckets**
- **Sifter (colander or sieve)**
- **Small Toys**

    particularly related to dinosaurs

Suggested Activities with New and Existing Materials:

Students can…

- participate in an archeological dig. They can use the tools available to find the "treasures" in the sand.
- place fossils made in the Science Center (page 107) in the dig.

New Materials:

• **Books**

ABC T-Rex by Bernard Most (Harcourt, 2000)

Dinosaur Bones by Bob Barner (Chronicle Books, 2001)

Suggested Activities with New and Existing Materials:

Students can…

• build a dinosaur with blocks. Encourage students to refer to the books in the center for construction and extension ideas.

• represent their structures on graph paper or blank paper. Post representations in the center.

SCIENCE CENTER

New Materials:

• **Magnifying Glasses**
• **Clay**
• **Crayons**
• **Plaster of Paris**
• **Empty, Clean Pint (250 ml) Milk Cartons**
• **Sea Shells**
• **Rocks**
• **Sticks**
• **Leaves**
• **Plastic Dinosaurs**

Suggested Activities with New and Existing Materials:

Students can…

• make fossils of things found in nature (shells, twigs, leaves, etc.).

• make fossils of dinosaur tracks (just press the feet of the plastic dinosaurs into the Plaster of Paris)

• Cut the top off of the milk carton. Pour about 1" (2.5 cm) of Plaster of Paris in the bottom of the milk carton. Have each student press an object into the plaster and pull it straight out so it leaves a clean impression. Let the fossils dry, then tear the milk carton off the plaster .

• make clay impressions and crayon rubbings of the completed fossils.

• sort fossils by size, shape, living, non-living, extinct, and not extinct.

MATH CENTER

New Materials:

• **Shapes of Various Dinosaurs**
• **Plastic Dinosaurs**
• **Data for Collection and Graphing—Students' Favorite Dinosaurs**
• **Jar Filled with "Dinosaur Eggs" (Jelly Beans)**
• **Box for Guesses**

Suggested Activities with New and Existing Materials:

Students can…

• make patterns with the shapes of dinosaurs. Have students record their patterns.

• sort and classify plastic dinosaurs by size, shape, plant-eater, meat-eater, etc.

- interview the other students in the center to determine their favorite dinosaurs. Students should make favorite dinosaur graphs.

- estimate the number of "dinosaur eggs" in the jar. Each student should write his name and estimate on a piece of paper and place it in the box for guesses. When the "eggs" are counted at the end of the unit, the class can see whose estimate came the closest.

ART CENTER

New Materials:
- **Books**

    1-2-3 *Draw Dinosaurs and Other Prehistoric Animals* by Freddie Levin (Peel Productions, 2001)

    Ed Emberley's Drawing Book of Animals by Ed Emberley (Little, Brown and Company, 1994)

- **Tables for Display**
- **Craft Paper for Backdrops**

Suggested Activities with New and Existing Materials:

Students can...

- make dinosaurs from recyclable materials.

- paint and/or draw dinosaurs.

- make dinosaurs from clay.

- place dinosaurs on murals or tables to create habitats. Students can use the craft paper for backdrops in their habitats.

Theme Materials & Activities

Themes may last for two to four weeks. You may choose to have some theme centers, as well as some month-by-month centers.

Reading | Writing | Home Living | Community | Blocks | Science | Math | Art

READING CENTER

New Materials:
- **Books**

    Barn by Debby Atwell (Houghton Mifflin, 2001)

    Big Red Barn by Margaret Wise Brown (HarperCollins, 1989)

    Click, Clack, Moo: Cows That Type by Doreen Cronin (Simon & Schuster, Inc., 2000)

    Farm Animals, Eye Openers by Angela Royston (Penguin Books Ltd., 1999)

    Farmer Brown Goes Round and Round by Teri Sloat (Dorling Kindersley Publishing, 2001)

    Horse in the Pigpen by Linda Williams (HarperCollins, 2002)

    Louella Mae, She's Run Away! by Karen Beaumont Alarcon (Henry Holt and Company, Inc., 2002)

    The Milk Makers by Gail Gibbons (Aladdin Library, 1987)

    Old MacDonald Had a Farm by Carol Jones (Houghton Mifflin, 1998)

    On Grandpa's Farm by Vivian Sathre (Houghton Mifflin, 1997)

    Our Animal Friends at Maple Hill Farm by Alice and Martin Provensen (Aladdin Library, 2001)

    Pigs by Gail Gibbons (Holiday House, 2000)

    Rosie's Walk by Pat Hutchins (Scott Foresman, 1971)

    Sally Goes to the Farm by Stephen Huneck (Harry N. Abrams, Inc., 2002)

    Twist and Ernest by Laura Barnes (Barnesyard Books, Inc., 2000)

- **Purchased Tapes/CDs**

    Rosie's Walk by Pat Hutchins (Weston Woods Studios, 1972)

- **Teacher-Made Tapes**

    Any story or book you read aloud (recorded while being read)

- **Predictable Chart**

    "At the Farm" (See page 27 for more information on predictable charts.)

    - Charts with sentences
    - Cards for sentence building
    - Class books

- **Flying Cow Wand for Reading the Room**

    A small cow-with-wings shape attached to the end of a yardstick or pointer

- **Any Stuffed Toy Farm Animals for Reading Buddies**

- **Barn for the Special Reading Place**

    Make a barn outline using craft paper, or, if possible, cover a large box (from a washing machine or dryer) to make a barn reading space. Place pillows in or near the barn.

Suggested Activities with New and Existing Materials:

Students can…

- read the books in the center to themselves or to the reading buddies, with emphasis on the farm animal books.

- listen to the new stories on tape, with emphasis on the farm animal stories.

- complete and read the predictable chart made during the Farm Animals unit.

- read the room with the flying cow wand. This activity can be done individually or in pairs.

- read in the Special Reading Place.

New Materials:

- **Books**

  Old MacDonald Had a Farm by Carol Jones (Houghton Mifflin, 1998)

  Our Animal Friends at Maple Hill Farm by Alice and Martin Provensen (Aladdin Library, 2001)

- **Farm Animals Picture Dictionary Chart**

  This is a chart with familiar farm animal words and pictures such as cow, chicken, horse, pig, tractor, farmer, etc.

- **Animal Shape Books—Cow, Pig, Barn**

  You will find the shapes of a cow, pig, and barn on pages 142 and 143. You will need to cut blank paper to match. Each book should have 4-5 blank pages.

- **Shape Stamps—Farm Animals**
- **Clipboard**

Suggested Activities with New and Existing Materials:

Students can…

- write a retelling of a farm animal story you have read aloud previously or a story they already know. Completed stories may be placed in the Reading Center.
- make a farm animals picture dictionary.
- write the room.

HOME LIVING CENTER

New Materials:
- **Empty Gallon (4 L) Milk Jugs**
- **Empty Egg Cartons**
- **Flour Sack**
- **Butter Tubs**
- **Grocery Bags**

Suggested Activities with New and Existing Materials:

Students can…

- put away farm-related groceries.
- bake and cook with farm-related ingredients.
- sort kitchen items by farm/not farm.

COMMUNITY CENTER

Grocery Store

New Materials:
- **Food**

  Boxes, cans, bags
- **Grocery Bags**
- **Paper for Grocery Lists and Receipts**
- **Carts or Baskets**
- **Gardening Supplies**

Suggested Activities with New and Existing Materials:

Students can…

- go to the grocery store to buy food and home living supplies.
- work in the grocery store.

BLOCKS CENTER

New Materials:

- **Books**

    Barn by Debby Atwell (Houghton Mifflin, 1996)

    Big Red Barn by Margaret Wise Brown (HarperCollins, 1989)

    On Grandpa's Farm by Vivian Sathre (Houghton Mifflin, 1997)

Suggested Activities with New and Existing Materials:

Students can...

- build barns with blocks. Encourage students to refer to the books in the center for construction and extension ideas.

- represent their structures on graph paper or blank paper. Post representations in the center.

SCIENCE CENTER

New Materials:

- **Seeds**

    Any type of seed will work well. Radish seeds grow very quickly and don't require much space.

- **Cups—Plastic or Foam**
- **Dirt/Potting Soil**
- **Plastic Tablecloth**
- **Plastic Spoons**
- **Watering Can**
- **Heavy Whipping Cream**
- **Baby Food Jars**
- **Salt**

Suggested Activities with New and Existing Materials:

Students can...

- plant the seeds in cups. Encourage students to work on the plastic tablecloth and keep the dirt and watering can in that space.

    Note: Students should need minimal supervision with this activity. Although mixing the dirt might be a bit messy, there is nothing that can harm students or damage other materials.

- observe plant growth. Encourage students to record how much their plants have grown from visit to visit.

- make butter by filling about ½ of a baby food jar with whipping cream and adding a pinch of salt. Students should shake the cream vigorously for about 7-10 minutes or until the butter rises to the top.

MATH CENTER

New Materials:

- **Books**

    One Gray Mouse by Katherine Burton (Kids Can Press, 2002)

    One Little Mouse by Dori Chaconas (Viking Children's Books, 2002)

- **Shapes of Different Farm Animals in Various Colors**

- **Plastic Farm Animals**
- **Data for Collection and Graphing—Students' Favorite Farm Animals**
- **Jar Filled with Plastic Farm Animals**
- **Box for Guesses**

Suggested Activities with New and Existing Materials:

Students can…

- make patterns with shapes of farm animals. Have students record their patterns.

- sort and classify plastic farm animals by size, color, number of feet, etc.

- interview the other students in the center to determine their favorite farm animals. Students should make favorite farm animal graphs.

- estimate the number of plastic farm animals in the jar. Each student should write her name and estimate on a piece of paper and place it in the box for guesses. When the plastic farm animals are counted at the end of the unit, the class can see whose estimate came the closest.

ART CENTER

New materials:

- **Books**

    1-2-3 *Draw Pets and Farm Animals: A Step by Step Guide* by Freddie Levin (Peel Productions, 2000)

    Barnyard Banter by Denise Fleming (Henry Holt and Company, Inc., 2001)

    Ed Emberley's Drawing Book of Animals by Ed Emberley (Little, Brown and Company, 1994)

- **Tables for Display**
- **Craft Paper for Backdrops**

Suggested Activities with New and Existing Materials:

Students can…

- make farm animals from recyclable materials.

- paint and/or draw farm animals.

- make farm animals from clay.

- place farm animals on mural or tables to create a barnyard scene.

Theme Materials & Activities

Themes may last for two to four weeks. You may choose to have some theme centers, as well as some month-by-month centers.

| Reading | Writing | Home Living | Community | Blocks | Science | Math | Art |

READING CENTER

New Materials:

- **Books**

  In the Small, Small Pond by Denise Fleming (Henry Holt and Company, Inc., 1998)

  It Could Still Be Water by Allan Fowler (Children's Book Press, 1993)

  Maisy's Pool by Lucy Cousins (Candlewick Press, 1999)

  My Duck by Tanya Linch (Bloomsbury Publishing, 2001)

  No More Water in the Tub! by Tedd Arnold (Puffin Books, 2002)

  Tuck in the Pool by Martha Weston (Houghton Mifflin, 2000)

  Water Dance by Thomas Locker (Voyager Books, 2002)

- **Purchased Tapes/CDs**

  In the Small, Small Pond by Denise Fleming (Henry Holt and Company, Inc., 1993)

- **Teacher-Made Tapes**

  Any story or book you read aloud (recorded while being read)

- **Sentence Strips for Interactive Chart**

  "Water" (See page 27 for more information on interactive charts.)

- **Predictable Charts**

  "Water," "At the Beach," "If I Am Thirsty I Drink" (See page 27 for more information on predictable charts.)

- Charts with sentences
- Cards for sentence building
- Class books

- **Fish Wand for Reading the Room**

  A fish shape attached to the end of a pointer or yardstick or an old fish-shaped oven mitt

- **Stuffed Toy Water Animals for Reading Buddies**

  Fish, salamanders, turtles, etc.

- **Small Plastic Wading Pool for the Special Reading Place**

  Add pillows for students to sit and read.

Suggested Activities with New and Existing Materials:

Students can...

- read the books in the center to themselves or to the reading buddies, with emphasis on the water books.

- listen to the stories on tape, with emphasis on the water stories.

- complete and read the interactive charts and predictable charts made during the Water unit.

- read the room with the fish wand. This activity can be done individually or in pairs.

- read in the Special Reading Place.

WRITING CENTER

New Materials:

- **Books**

  My Duck by Tanya Linch (Bloomsbury Publishing, 2000)

- **Water Picture Dictionary Chart**

  This is a chart with familiar water words and pictures such as water, rain, drops, puddles, pools, rivers, streams, beach, etc.

- **Water Shape Books—Watering Can, Water Drop**

  You will find the shape of a watering can and a water drop on pages 143 and 144. Once you determine what shape you will use, cut blank paper to match. Each book should have 4-5 blank pages.

- **Shape Stamps—Umbrellas, Water Drops**

- **Clipboard**

Suggested Activities with New and Existing Materials:

Students can…

- write a retelling of a water story you have read aloud previously or a story they already know. Completed stories may be placed in the Reading Center.

- make a water picture dictionary

- write a story about a time they were in the water.

- write the room.

HOME LIVING CENTER

New Materials:

- **Tub of Water for Washing**

- **Washcloths**

- **Anti-Bacterial Dish Soap**

Suggested Activities with New and Existing Materials:

Students can…

- wash the dishes, tables, etc., to keep the home living center clean. Encourage students to wash plastic babies and their toys. If possible allow students to wash and line dry baby clothing.

COMMUNITY CENTER

Toy Company Specializing in Water Toys

New Materials:

- **Small Child's Wading Pool with Water**

- **Water Toys**

- **Corks**

- **Plastic Butter Tubs with Lids**

- **Other Floating Materials**

- **Decorative Materials**

  Feathers, yarn balls, eyes, etc.

- **Optional: Baby Food Jars with Lids, Glitter, and Small Objects**

  For example, holiday shapes, seashells, etc.

- **Optional: Waterproof Glue**

Suggested Activities with New and Existing Materials:

Students can...

- begin their work by playing with toys that other people have already made (market research).

- design water toys using floating materials and decorations. Students should be encouraged to use what they learned in the Science Center about what sinks and floats. They should also be encouraged to think about what makes toys interesting (appearance, color, size, shape, etc.).

- try out their inventions before placing them on display. Displays should have "place" cards with the name of the invention, the name of the inventor and a brief description of the invention.

- make snow globes (optional). Glue objects (plastic houses, snow men, animals, etc.) to the lid of the baby food jar with waterproof glue. Add water and a teaspoon of glitter to each jar. Seal tightly (you may want to use more waterproof glue or a hot glue gun), turn over, and shake.

BLOCKS CENTER

New Materials:

- **Books**

    Maisy's Pool by Lucy Cousins (Candlewick Press, 1999)

    Tuck in the Pool by Martha Weston (Houghton Mifflin, 2000)

Suggested Activities with New and Existing Materials:

Students can...

- build swimming pools with blocks. Encourage students to refer to the books in the center for construction and extension ideas.

- represent their structures on graph paper or blank paper. Post representations in the center.

SCIENCE CENTER

New Materials:

- **Diatomaceous Earth**

    Diatomaceous earth is a white, soil-like substance made from the ground shells of the skeletal remains of diatoms, a microscopic form of algae. When water is poured on Diatomaceous earth, streams and crevices are formed. Diatomaceous earth is a fully inert, non-volatile substance that has proven effective in eradicating certain pests. It is also used as a filter in a swimming pool filtration system. You want the Diatomaceous earth used in filtering systems. It can be purchased at any swimming pool supply store. A 10 lb. bag should be about $15.

    To prepare the Diatomaceous earth for use, you will need to mix approximately 14 cups of water to 15 cups of earth. Wear a filter mask as the Diatomaceous earth is very dusty! Mix with a trowel or sturdy wooden spoon until wet. Test to see if it is ready by slightly raising one end of the tub (use a book or any other object that will support the tub and provide stability) and slowly pour water over the earth. If it is ready, the water will form a small stream and pool at the end of the tub. If it soaks in, it needs a bit more water and mixing. You will not need to "remix" the earth every day. Check once a week or so to see if it needs more water but it should not need any special treatment once it is mixed.

- **58 Quart/55 Liter Plastic Tub with Lid**

- **Watering Can**

- **Sticks and Rocks of Various Sizes**

- **Baster**

- **Sponges of Various Sizes and Materials**

    Be sure one is a natural sponge.

- **Clear Plastic Cups**

- **Various Objects that Sink or Float**

    Rocks, sponges, foam, paper clips, erasers, cork, etc.

- **Several Small Tubs of Water**

- **Water Log for Recording Results**

Suggested Activities with New and Existing Materials:

Students can...

- make observations about the Diatomaceous earth. Students should slowly pour water over the Diatomaceous earth. Encourage students to use the rocks and sticks to create diversions to the "streams" they are making. Don't forget to slightly elevate one end of the tub to create a downward slope. Students scoop up the Diatomaceous earth with their hands and reform the earth. When students have emptied one watering can they can collect the water with the baster and return it to the watering can, then begin again.

   Clean-up is easy. They should collect the water from the Diatomaceous earth with a baster and sponges. Diatomaceous earth washes off easily from hands and supplies. If the Diatomaceous earth gets on clothing, allow the clothing to dry and the diatomaceous earth will brush off like flour.

   Note: Students may need some supervision getting started with this activity, however they should become self-sufficient rather quickly. Although scooping the Diatomaceous earth might be a bit messy, there is nothing that can harm students or damage other materials.

- place sponges in the water one at time. Have students count to ten. They should squeeze the sponge out in a container. Each sponge should be tested in the same way with each being "squeezed" into a different container. Which one held the most water? Students should record their findings in the water log.

- test which objects sink in the water and which float. They should record their findings in the water log.

MATH CENTER

New Materials:

- **Raindrop Shapes of Various Sizes and Colors**
- **Data for Collection and Graphing—Students' Favorite Drinks**
- **Cup, Pint, and Quart Measures (250 ml, 500 ml, 1 L)**
   Empty milk containers work well
- **Pitchers of Water**
- **Large Tub to Hold Water**
- **Jar Filled with Cotton Balls**
- **Box for Guesses**

Suggested Activities with New and Existing Materials:

Students can...

- make patterns with raindrop shapes. Have students record their patterns.

- sort and classify raindrops by size, shape, and color.

- interview the other students in the center to determine their favorite drinks. They should make favorite drink graphs.

- determine how many cups (250 ml containers) are in a pint (500 ml container), how many cups (250 ml containers) are in a quart (1 L container), and how many pints (500 ml containers) are in a quart (1 L container) by pouring water from pitchers into measuring containers. Students should record equivalent measures.

- estimate the number of cotton balls in the jar. Each student should write his name and estimate on a piece of paper and place it in the box for guesses. When the cotton balls are counted at the end of the unit, the class can see whose estimate came the closest.

New Materials:

• **Book**

   Water Dance by Thomas Locker (Voyager Books, 2002)

• **Watercolor Paints**

Suggested Activities with New and Existing Materials:

Students can...

- make rain pictures with watercolors.

- paint and/or draw swimming pools, rivers, and streams. Encourage students to use the reference materials in the center as they create their paintings.

Theme Materials & Activities

Themes may last for two to four weeks. You may choose to have some theme centers, as well as some month-by-month centers.

| Reading | Writing | Home Living | Community | Blocks | Science | Math | Art |

READING CENTER

New Materials:

• **Books**

Caps, Hats, Socks and Mittens: A Book About the Four Seasons by Louise Borden (Scholastic, Inc., 1992)

The Cloud Book by Tomie De Paola (Holiday House, 1985)

Cloud Dance by Thomas Locker (Voyager Books, 2003)

Cloudy with a Chance of Meatballs by Judi Barrett (Aladdin Library, 1982)

Come On, Rain! by Karen Hesse (Scholastic, Inc., 1999)

Is The Sky Always Blue? by Eric Adler (Kansas City Star Books, 2002)

The Jacket I Wear in the Snow by Shirley Neitzel (HarperTrophy, 1994)

Rain by Robert Kalan (HarperTrophy, 1991)

Rain Rain Rivers by Uri Shulevitz (Farrar, Straus and Giroux, 1988)

Small Cloud by Ariane (Walker & Company, 1996)

The Snowman by Raymond Briggs (Random House, 1987)

The Snowy Day by Ezra Jack Keats (Puffin Books, 1981)

The Storm Book by Charlotte Zolotow (HarperTrophy, 1989)

• **Purchased Tapes/CDs**

The Snowy Day by Ezra Jack Keats (Kimbo Educational Audio, 1984)

• **Teacher-Made Tapes**

Any story or book you read aloud (recorded while being read)

• **Sentence Strips for Interactive Charts**

"Winter," "Spring," "Summer," "Fall" (See page 27 for more information on interactive charts.)

• **Predictable Charts**

"In Fall," "In Winter," "In Spring," "Weather" (See page 27 for more information on predictable charts.)

  • Charts with sentences
  • Cards for sentence building
  • Class books

• **Lightning Bolt Wand for Reading the Room**

A zig-zag shaped piece of cardboard wrapped in aluminum foil and attached to the end of a pointer or yardstick

• **Soft Dolls or Toy Stuffed Animals Dressed for the Weather for Reading Buddies**

Or any other weather-related stuffed object (cloud, raindrop, sun, etc.)

• **Large Umbrella for the Special Reading Place**

Hang a large umbrella over a part of the Reading Center. If possible, hang it rather low so students feel like they are reading under the umbrella. You can also make an igloo. (See page 135 for directions.)

Suggested Activities with New and Existing Materials:

Students can…

• read the books in the center to themselves or to the reading buddies, with emphasis on the weather books.

• listen to the stories on tape, with emphasis on the weather stories.

• complete and read the interactive charts and predictable charts made during the Weather unit.

- read the room with the lightening bolt wand. This activity can be done individually or in pairs.

- read in the Special Reading Place.

WRITING CENTER

New materials:

- **Books**

    Caps, Hats, Socks and Mittens: A Book About the Four Seasons by Louise Borden (Scholastic, Inc., 1992)

    Is The Sky Always Blue? by Eric Adler (Kansas City Star Books, 2002)

    The Cloud Book by Tomie De Paola (Holiday House, 1985)

- **Weather Picture Dictionary Chart**

    This is a chart with familiar weather words and pictures such as rain, sun, snow, sleet, sunny, cloudy, tornado, hurricane, etc.

- **Weather Shape Books—Snowman, Umbrella, Sun, and Cloud**

    You can make the outline of the shape or you can purchase large shaped notepads from your local school supply store. You will find a cloud shape on page 144. Once you determine what shape you will

use, cut blank paper to match. Each book should have 4-5 blank pages.

- **Shape Stamps—Snowman, Umbrella, Cloud, Sun**
- **Clipboard**

Suggested Activities with New and Existing Materials:

Students can...

- write retellings of weather stories you have read aloud previously or stories they already know. Completed stories may be placed in the Reading Center.

- make a weather picture dictionary.

- write stories about times they were out in the weather, scared by the weather, or really enjoyed the weather.

- write the room.

HOME LIVING CENTER

New Materials:
- **Travel Magazines**
- **Suitcases**
- **Travel Bags**
- **Shaving and Toiletries Bags**
- **Empty Shampoo Bottles**
- **Brushes**
- **Clothing Suited for Various Climates**

Suggested Activities with New and Existing Materials:

Students can...

- pack for a variety of "vacations." Students should be able to tell where they are going, what they will do when they get there, and what they need to take with them. The vacations will be arranged through the Travel Agency (Community Center, page 120).

Travel Agency

New Materials:

- **Travel Brochures**
- **Maps**
- **Travel Books**
- **Cameras**
- **Travel Posters**
- **Postcards**

Suggested Activities with New and Existing Materials:

Students can…

- plan a variety of vacations. Students should determine where they want to go based on the climate of the destinations. Encourage students to refer to the postcards, travel brochures, books, and posters as they plan.

- work in the travel agency to help others plan vacations.

BLOCKS CENTER

New Materials:

- **Books**

    Bear At Home by Stella Blackstone (Barefoot Books, 2001)

    Building a House by Byron Barton (William Morrow, 1981)

    Houses and Homes by Ann Morris (HarperTrophy, 1995)

Suggested Activities with New and Existing Materials:

Students can…

- build places with blocks where they would be safe from bad weather. Encourage students to refer to the books in the center for construction and extension ideas.

- represent their structures on graph paper or blank paper. Post representations in the center.

SCIENCE CENTER

New materials:

- **Book**

    What Makes A Rainbow? by Betty Schwartz (Intervisual Books, Inc., 2000)

- **Thermometer**
- **Weather Chart**
- **Shaving Cream**
- **Red, Blue, and Yellow Tempera Paint**
- **Resealable Plastic Sandwich Bags**
- **Several Small Containers (Butter Tub Size)**
- **Paintbrushes**
- **White Paper**

Suggested Activities with New and Existing Materials:

Students can…

- read the thermometer and record the daily temperature on a chart in the center.

- record weather conditions (for example, cloudy, sunny, etc.) on the chart.

- make a rainbow. Encourage students to refer to resources in the room to determine what colors they will need and how they will place them on their rainbow. Students should be encouraged to create all six primary and secondary colors.

    Students should mix their secondary colors in small containers using a paintbrush, or they can mix their secondary colors in resealable plastic bags with a squirt of shaving cream (shaving cream serves as mixing agent and dries clear). If mixing in resealable plastic bags, start with a squirt of shaving cream. Add tempera paint. Seal the bag well and gently massage the paint into the shaving cream.

Once colors are created, students can make their own rainbows on the white paper.

MATH CENTER

New Materials:

- **Books**

   Fish Eyes by Lois Ehlert (Voyager Books, 1992)

   The Baseball Counting Book by Barbara McGrath (Charlesbridge Publishing, 1999)

- **Snowman, Umbrella, Sun, and Cloud Shapes of Various Colors**
- **Umbrellas of Various Colors and Sizes**
- **Yardsticks**
- **Jar Filled with Small Paper Umbrellas**

   Usually found in drinks

- **Box for Guesses**

Suggested Activities with New and Existing Materials:

Students can…

- make patterns with snowman, umbrella, sun, and cloud shapes. Have students record their patterns.
- sort and classify umbrellas by color and size.
- measure the umbrellas using the yardsticks. Students should record the measurements.
- estimate the number of paper umbrellas in the jar. Each student should write his name and estimate on a piece of paper, and place it in the box for guesses. When the paper umbrellas are counted at the end of the unit, the class can see whose estimate came the closest.

ART CENTER

New Materials:

- **Books**

   How Artists See the Weather by Colleen Carroll (Abbeville Press, Inc., 1998)

   An Island in the Sun by Stella Blackstone (Barefoot Books, 2003)

- **Black Water Wash**

   Black watercolor paint in a large amount of water

- **Blue Water Wash**

   Blue watercolor paint in a large amount of water

- **Magazines**

Suggested Activities with New and Existing Materials:

Students can…

- make umbrellas using recyclables materials. Have students write the directions for making their umbrellas.
- paint and/or draw two matching pictures. Use the black water wash on one to create a cloudy day and the blue water wash on the other to create a sunny day. Encourage students to label their pictures.
- cut out magazine pictures that show different weather conditions, seasons, etc. Encourage students to label their pictures.

Living & Non-Living
Theme Materials & Activities

Themes may last for two to four weeks. You may choose to have some theme centers, as well as some month-by-month centers.

| Reading | Writing | Home Living | Community | Blocks | Science | Math | Art |

READING CENTER

New materials:

- **Books**

    Eating the Alphabet: Fruits and Vegetables from A to Z by Lois Ehlert (Voyager Books, 1993)

    Eric Carle's Animals Animals by Eric Carle (Puffin Books, 1999)

    Everybody Needs a Rock by Byrd Baylor (Scott Foresman, 1985)

    A House for Hermit Crab by Eric Carle (Aladdin Library, 2002)

    Inch by Inch by Leo Lionni (HarperTrophy, 1995)

    It Could Still Be a Rock by Allan Fowler (Children's Book Press, 1993)

    Living Things by Judith Holloway (Modern Curriculum Press, 1993)

    The Mixed-Up Chameleon by Eric Carle (HarperTrophy, 1988)

    Rocks in His Head by Carol Otis Hurst (Greenwillow Books, 2001)

    The Tiny Seed by Eric Carle (Aladdin Library, 2001)

    Worms Wiggle by David Pelham (Little Simon, 1989)

- **Teacher-Made tapes**

    Any story or book you read aloud (recorded while being read)

- **Sentence Strips for Interactive Chart**

    "Rocks" (See page 27 for more information on interactive charts.)

- **Predictable Chart**

    "Living and Non-Living" (See page 27 for more information on predictable charts.)

    - Charts with sentences
    - Cards for sentence building
    - Class books

- **A Horseshoe Magnet Wand for Reading the Room**

    A horseshoe magnet attached to the end of a pointer or yardstick

- **"Pet Rocks" Students Make in the Art Center**

    See page 125.

- **Large Craft Paper Tree for the Special Reading Place**

    Twist brown craft paper to make limbs. Cut green paper to make large canopy of leaves. Make the tree low to the ground so students feel they are reading under the tree. Include some seating made of wood—benches, chairs, etc. Identify that some living things are used when they are no longer living.

Suggested Activities with New and Existing Materials:

Students can…

- read the books in the center to themselves or to the reading buddies, with emphasis on the living/non-living books.

- listen to the stories on tape, with emphasis on the living/non-living stories.

- complete and read the interactive charts and predictable charts made during the Living & Non-Living unit.

- read the room with the horseshoe magnet wand. This activity can be done individually or in pairs.

- read in the Special Reading Place.

New Materials:

- **Books**

  Eric Carle's Animals, Animals by Eric Carle (Puffin. 1999)

  Everybody Needs a Rock by Byrd Baylor (Scott Foresman, 1985)

  The Tiny Seed by Eric Carle (Aladdin Library, 2001)

- **Living and Non-Living Picture Dictionary Chart**

  This is a chart with familiar "living and non-living" words and pictures such as living, non-living, rocks, plants, animals, magnets, etc.

- **Shape Books—Rock, Worm, Beetle, Tree**

  You will find rock, worm, and beetle shapes on pages 145-146 You will find a tree shape on page 141. Once you determine what shape you will use, cut blank paper to match. Each book should have 4-5 blank pages.

- **Shape Stamps—Plant, Rock, Worm, Beetle**

- **Clipboard**

Suggested Activities with New and Existing Materials:

Students can…

- write a retelling of a living and non-living story you have read aloud previously or a story they already know. Completed stories may be placed in the Reading Center.

- make a living and non-living picture dictionary.

- write the room.

New Materials:

- **Live Plants**

- **Live Animal**

  Fish, small mammal (such as gerbil), small reptile (such as lizard), small amphibian (such as frog or toad)

Suggested Activities with New and Existing Materials:

Students can…

- place the new living things in appropriate places in the Home Living Center. Students should make lists of what is needed to care for the living things, as well as write directions on how to care for the living things.

Repair Shop

New Materials:

- **Old Appliances with Electrical Cords Removed**

  Curling irons, toasters, tape recorders, etc.

- **Screwdrivers**

- **Pliers**

- **Muffin Tins**

- **Aprons or Denim Shirts**

Suggested Activities with New and Existing Materials:

Students can…

- work in the repair shop. Workers can take appliances apart and sort the parts (screws, springs, gears, etc.) in muffin tins. Sorted items go to the recyclables in the Art Center at the end of the unit.

- send or pick up appliances from the repair shop.

BLOCKS CENTER

New Materials:

- **Books**

  Block City by Robert Louis Stevenson (Puffin Books, 1992)

  City: A Story of Roman Planning and Construction by David MacAulay (Houghton Mifflin/Walter Lorraine Books, 1983)

Suggested Activities with New and Existing Materials:

Students can...

- build cities with blocks. Encourage students to refer to the books in the center for construction and extension ideas.

- represent their structures on graph paper or blank paper. Students should identify the living and non-living things in the pictures. Post representations in the center.

SCIENCE CENTER

New Materials:

- **Plants**
- **Seeds**
- **Any Classroom Pets**
- **Various Rocks**
- **Various Metallic Items**
- **Scientist's Log**

  Fold several blank pieces of paper, place them inside a folded piece of construction paper, and staple the folded edges to form a book. You can make one log per child or a larger, class log where everyone can record their findings.

Suggested Activities with New and Existing Materials:

Students can...

- sort new materials into living and non-living categories.

- sort and classify rocks by size, shape, hardness, and color.

- test, sort, and record objects that are attracted and not attracted to a magnet. Students should test the walls, tables, and chairs within the center. Students should record their observations in a Scientist's Log.

- determine how plants and animals are the same and how they are different. Students should draw pictures to show the difference.

MATH CENTER

New Materials:

- **Books**

  Dogs, Dogs, Dogs! by Leslea Newman (Simon & Schuster, Inc., 2002)

  Ten Dogs in the Window: A Countdown Book by Claire Masurel (North South Books, 1997)

- **Rocks of Various Sizes, Shapes, and Colors**

- **Magazines**
- **4.25" x 5.5" (108 mm x 139.5 mm) Pieces of Paper—Photo Paper**

  ¼ sheets of copy paper

- **Scissors**
- **Glue**
- **Jar Filled with Rocks**
- **Box for Guesses**

Suggested Activities with New and Existing Materials:

Students can...

- make patterns with rocks. Have students record their patterns.

- sort and classify pictures of plants found in magazines. Students should glue individual pictures on pieces of photo paper and leave in the center for other students to use.

- weigh rocks. Student should record weights.

- estimate the number of rocks in the jar. Each student should write her name and estimate on a piece of paper, and place it in the box for guesses. When the rocks are counted at the end of the unit, the class can see whose estimate came the closest.

ART CENTER

New Materials:

- **Books**

    The Wing on A Flea: A Book About Shapes by Ed Emberley (Little, Brown and Company, 2001)

Suggested Activities with New and Existing Materials:

Students can...

- make sculptures from recyclables and rocks.

- paint rocks to look like faces or animals. Encourage students to use the reference materials in the center. These are their "pet rock" reading buddies for the Reading Center (page 122).

- draw and paint pictures of the plants or animals in the Science Center.

Theme Materials & Activities

Themes may last for two to four weeks. You may choose to have some theme centers, as well as some month-by-month centers.

| Reading | Writing | Home Living | Community | Blocks | Science | Math | Art |

READING CENTER

New Materials:

- **Books**

    The Big Orange Splot by Daniel Pinkwater (Scholastic, Inc., 1993)

    A Color of His Own by Leo Lionni (Dragonfly, 1997)

    Freight Train by Donald Crews (HarperTrophy, 1992)

    Mary Wore Her Red Dress and Henry Wore His Green Sneakers by Merle Peek (Houghton Mifflin, 1998)

    Mouse Paint by Ellen Stoll Walsh (Voyager Books, 1995)

    My Many Colored Days by Dr. Seuss (Knopf, 1998)

    Of Colors and Things by Tana Hoban (HarperTrophy, 1996)

    Red Leaf, Yellow Leaf by Lois Ehlert (Harcourt Children's Books, 1991)

    What Makes A Rainbow? by Betty Schwartz (Intervisual Books, Inc., 2000)

- **Purchased Tapes/CDs**

    Mary Wore Her Red Dress and Henry Wore His Green Sneakers by Merle Peek (Clarion Books, 1993)

    Freight Train by Donald Crews (William Morrow & Company, 1992)

- **Teacher-Made Tapes**

    Any book or story you read aloud (recorded while being read)

- **Sentence Strips for Interactive Charts**

    "The Flowerpot," "Mary Wore Her Red Dress," "What Is It?," "Crayons," "Rainbows" (See page 27 for more information on interactive charts.)

- **Predictable Charts**

    "My Head Is Full of Colors," "Green Eggs and Ham" (See page 27 for more information on predictable charts.)

    - Charts with sentences
    - Cards for sentence building
    - Class books

- **A Rainbow Wand for reading the room**

    A small rainbow attached to the end of a pointer or yardstick

- **Bright, Colorful Toy Stuffed Animals for Reading Buddies**

- **Rainbow for the Special Reading Place**

    Hang a rainbow over one corner of the reading center. Place the rainbow low so students feel as if they are reading under the rainbow.

Suggested Activities with New and Existing Materials:

Students can…

- read the books in the center to themselves or to the reading buddies, with emphasis on colors books.

- listen to the stories on tape, with emphasis on the colors stories.

- complete and read the interactive charts and predictable charts made during the Colors unit.

- read the room with the rainbow wand. This activity can be done individually or in pairs.

- read in the Special Reading Place.

WRITING CENTER

New Materials:

- **Books**

  Mary Wore Her Red Dress and Henry Wore His Green Sneakers by Merle Peek (Houghton Mifflin, 1998)

- **Colors Picture Dictionary Chart**

  This is a chart with familiar color words and pictures such as red, orange, yellow, green, blue, purple, rainbow, etc.

- **Shape Book—Rainbow**

  You will find a rainbow shape on page 146. You will need to cut blank paper to match the rainbow cover. Each book should have 4-5 blank pages.

- **Shape Stamps—Rainbow, Paint Bucket**
- **Clipboard**

Suggested Activities with New and Existing Materials:

Students can...

- write a retelling of a colors story you have read aloud previously or a story they already know. Completed stories may be placed in the Reading Center.
- make a colors picture dictionary.
- write a story about their favorite colors.
- write the room.

HOME LIVING CENTER

New Materials:

- **2-9 Small Laundry Baskets**
- **Clothing of Various Colors**

Suggested Activities with New Materials:

Students can...

- sort clothing and home living items by color. If two baskets are used they can sort by whites and colors. If more than two baskets are used they can sort by color (red, orange, yellow, green, blue, purple, brown, black, white). When "laundry" is done, students should put clean clothing away.

COMMUNITY CENTER

Highway Department

New Materials:

- **Books**

  The Big Red Bus by Judy Hindley (Candlewick Press, 2000)

  Cars by Anne Rockwell (Puffin Books, 1992)

  Richard Scarry's Cars and Trucks and Things That Go by Richard Scarry (Van Nostrand Reinhold, 1974)

  Round Trip by Ann Jonas (HarperTrophy, 1990)

  School Buses by Dee Ready (Bridgestone Books, 1997)

  Trash Trucks by Daniel Kirk (Putnam Publishing Group, 1997)

  Truck by Donald Crews (HarperTrophy, 1991)

  The Wheels on the Bus by Paul O. Zelinsky (Dutton Books, 1990)

- **Posters of Road Signs**
- **Yellow Tape**
- **White Tape**
- **Poster Board**
- **Paint**
- **Markers**
- **Glue**

- **Packing Tape**
- **Several Yardsticks**

    Or other long, narrow pieces of wood

- **Several Buckets Filled with Beans or Small Rocks**

Suggested Activities with New and Existing Materials:

Students can…

- make road markings on the floor of the center, road signs, and anything else they can think of related to highway safety. Completed road signs should be attached to yardsticks and placed in the buckets of beans/rocks. Encourage students to refer to the books in the center as resources and references.

BLOCKS CENTER

New Materials:

- **Books**

    Freight Train by Donald Crews (HarperTrophy, 1992)

    All Aboard Trains by Mary Harding (Grosset & Dunlap, 1989)

    Country Crossing by Jim Aylesworth (Aladdin Library, 1995)

Suggested Activities with New and Existing Materials:

Students can…

- build trains and/or railroad tracks using blocks. Encourage students to refer to the books in the center for construction and extension ideas.

- represent their structures on graph paper or blank paper. Post representations in the center.

SCIENCE CENTER

New Materials:
- **White Carnations**
- **Celery**
- **Food Coloring**
- **Clear Vase or Glass**
- **Water**
- **Shaving Cream**
- **Red, Blue, and Yellow Tempera Paint**
- **Resealable Plastic Sandwich Bags**
- **Several Small Containers (Butter Tub Size)**
- **Paintbrushes**
- **White Paper**

Suggested Activities with New and Existing Materials:

Students can…

- watch what happens when plants are placed in colored water. They should note which plant absorbed the colored water faster.

    Take one celery stalk and bend it until it splits, but doesn't break in half. This should form an upside down V. Place one half of the V in a glass of colored water and the other half in a glass of different colored water. Students should note what happens when the two colors meet in the middle of the celery stalk.

- make color wheels.

    Encourage students to refer to resources in the room to determine what colors they will need and how they will place them on their color wheels. Students should mix secondary colors in small containers with paintbrushes, or they can mix the colors in resealable plastic bags with a squirt of shaving cream (shaving cream serves as mixing agent and dries clear). If mixing in resealable plastic bags, start with a squirt of shaving cream. Then, add tempera paint. Seal the bag well and gently massage the paint into the shaving cream.

    Once the colors are created, students can make their own color wheels on the white paper.

New Materials:

- **Books**

  One Gray Mouse by Katherine Burton (Kids Can Press, 2002)

  Ten Red Apples by Pat Hutchins (Greenwillow Books, 2000)

- **Pattern Cubes**
- **Crayons**
- **Data for Collection and Graphing—Students' Favorite Colors**
- **Jelly Beans**
- **Jar Filled with Jelly Beans**
- **Box for Guesses**

Suggested Activities with New and Existing Materials:

Students can…

- make patterns with pattern cubes and/or jelly beans. Have students record their patterns.
- sort and classify crayons by size and shape.
- interview other students in the center to determine their favorite colors. Students should make favorite colors graphs.
- estimate the number of jelly beans in the jar. Each student should write his name and estimate on a piece of paper and place it in the box for guesses. When the jelly beans are counted at the end of the unit, the class can see whose estimate came the closest.

ART CENTER

New Materials:

- **Books**

  A Child's Book of Art: Discover Great Paintings by Lucy Micklethwait (Dorling Kindersley Publishing, 1999)

Suggested Activities with New and Existing Materials:

Students can…

- make whatever they want. Encourage students to use a variety of colors and to mix the colors they use.

Shaving cream is a fun and inexpensive way to clean tables and counter tops. Squirt shaving cream and let children "finger paint." When dry, wipe clean with a damp cloth or sponge.

Transportation

Theme Materials & Activities

Themes may last for two to four weeks. You may choose to have some theme centers, as well as some month-by-month centers.

Reading Writing Home Living Community Blocks Science Math Art

READING CENTER

New Materials:

• **Books**

Airport by Byron Barton (HarperTrophy, 1987)

All Aboard ABC by Doug Magee and Robert Newman (Cobblehill, 1990)

The Big Red Bus by Judy Hindley (Candlewick Press, 2000)

Car Wash by Sandra Steen and Susan Steen (Puffin Books, 2003)

Cars by Anne Rockwell (Puffin Books, 1992)

Freight Train by Donald Crews (HarperTrophy, 1992)

I Love Trains! by Philemon Sturges (HarperTrophy, 2003)

Lisa's Airplane Trip by Anne Gutman and Georg Hallensleben (Knopf, 2001)

The Little Engine That Could by Watty Piper (Grosset & Dunlap, 1978)

Next Stop Grand Central by Maira Kalman (Puffin Books, 2001)

Planes by Anne Rockwell (Puffin Books, 1993)

Richard Scarry's Cars and Trucks and Things That Go by Richard Scarry (Van Nostrand Reinhold, 1974)

Round Trip by Ann Jonas (HarperTrophy, 1990)

School Buses by Dee Ready (Bridgestone Books, 1997)

Trains by Anne Rockwell (Puffin Books, 1993)

Trash Trucks by Daniel Kirk (Putnam Publishing Group, 1997)

Truck by Donald Crews (HarperTrophy, 1991)

Two Little Trains by Margaret Wise Brown (Harpercollins Juvenile Books, 2003)

The Wheels on the Bus by Paul O. Zelinsky (Dutton Books, 1990)

• **Purchased Tapes/CDs**

Freight Train by Donald Crews (William Morrow & Company, 1992)

• **Teacher-Made Tapes**

Any book or story you read aloud (recorded while being read)

• **Sentence Strips for Interactive Chart**

"Transportation" (See page 27 for more information on interactive charts.)

• **Predictable Chart**

"The Little Engine that Could" (See page 27 for more information on predictable charts.)

- Chart with sentences
- Cards for sentence building
- Class book

• **Car and/or Truck Wand for Reading the Room**

A car or truck shape attached to the end of a pointer or yardstick

• **Any Stuffed Toy Form of Transportation for Reading Buddies**

A truck, bus, car, train, etc.

• **Car, Bus, Train, and/or Plane for the Special Reading Place**

Make a vehicle in the center by taping off an area and placing chairs within that area.

Suggested Activities with New and Existing Materials:

Students can...

- read the books in the center to themselves or to the reading buddies, with emphasis on the transportation books.

- listen to the stories on tape, with emphasis on the transportation stories.
- complete and read the interactive charts and predictable charts made during the Transportation unit.

- read the room with the car and/or truck wand. This activity can be done individually or in pairs.
- read in the Special Reading Place.

WRITING CENTER

New Materials:

- **Books**

    I Love Trains! by Philemon Sturges (HarperTrophy, 2003)

    The Wheels on the Bus by Paul O. Zelinsky (Dutton Books, 1990)

- **Transportation Picture Dictionary Chart**

    This is a chart with familiar transportation words and pictures such as car, truck, plane, bus, trip, road, tracks, runways, etc.

- **Transportation Shape Books—Bus, Car, Airplane, etc.**

    You can make the outline of the shape or you can purchase large shaped notepads from your local school supply store. Once you determine what shape you will use, cut blank paper to match. Each book should have 4-5 blank pages.

- **Shape Stamps—Bus, Cars, Airplanes, etc.**
- **Clipboard**

Suggested Activities with New and Existing Materials:

Students can...

- write a retelling of a transportation story you have read aloud previously or a story they already know. Completed stories may be placed in the Reading Center.
- make a transportation picture dictionary.
- write a story about riding in or on their favorite transportation vehicle.
- write the room.

HOME LIVING CENTER

New Materials:
- **Catalogs, Newspaper Ads, Travel Brochures**
- **Suitcases**

Suggested Activities with New and Existing Materials:

Students can...

- plan and take vacations.
- pack for their trips.

COMMUNITY CENTER

Vehicles

New Materials:

- **Car, Bus, Train, and/or Plane**

    Create a mode of transportation using a box (or boxes) with chairs placed inside the box(es).

- **Clothing and Accessories for Drivers, Pilots, Flight Attendants, Conductors, Passengers, etc.**
    - Seat belts
    - Radio
    - Steering wheels
    - Horns
    - Tickets

Suggested Activities with New and Existing Materials:

Students can...

- decorate and make additions to the transportation vehicle(s). Encourage students to use the reference materials in the center to create a more "realistic" bus, train, etc.

- drive/pilot the transportation vehicle(s). Students should be able to tell where they are going and how they will get there.

- ride the transportation vehicle(s). Students should be able to tell where they are going and what they will do when they get there.

BLOCKS CENTER

New Materials:

- **Books**

  Bridges Are to Cross by Philemon Sturges (Puffin Books, 2000)

  Bridges Connect: A Building Block Book by Lee Sullivan Hill (Carolrhoda Books, 1996)

  New Road! by Gail Gibbons (Harpercollins Juvenile Books, 1983)

- **Small Toy Cars, Trucks, Trains, etc.**
- **Small Road Signs**
- **Small Model Trees**

Suggested Activities with New and Existing Materials:

Students can...

- build roads, train tracks, airports, train stations, etc. Encourage students to refer to the books in the center for construction and extension ideas.

- represent their structures on graph paper or blank paper. Post representations in the center.

SCIENCE CENTER

New Materials:

- **Window Facing a "Busy" Street**
- **Paper and Pencil**
- **Small Toy Cars of Various Sizes**
- **Flat, Thin Board**
- **Track for Toy Cars**
- **Books to Create an Incline for the Track**

Suggested Activities with New and Existing Materials:

Students can...

- observe the different types of transportation that pass by the school. Students should make categories and count the number of buses, cars, bikes, motorcycles, etc., that pass by while they are observing.

- observe the speed of different sizes of toy cars rolling down the flat, thin board. Students should record their observations and indicate why they think some of the cars are faster than others.

- observe the speed of a toy car rolling down the track at different angles of inclination. Students should record their observations and indicate whether the incline of the track makes the cars roll faster.

New Materials:

- **Books**

  One Duck Stuck by Phyllis Root (Candlewick Press, 2003)

- **Small Toy Cars**

  A variety of both metal and plastic

- **Various Pictures of Transportation**

  Cut outs and/or pictures of buses, trains, planes, etc.

- **Data for Collection and Graphing—How Students Get to School**

- **Jar Filled with Keys**

- **Box for Guesses**

Suggested activities with new and existing materials:

Students can…

- make patterns using small toy cars. Have students record their patterns.

- sort and classify pictures of transportation by size, shape, or type of transportation.

- interview other students in the center to determine how they get to school. Students should make school transportation graphs.

- estimate the number of keys in the jar. Each student should write his name and estimate on a piece of paper and place it in the box for guesses. When the keys are counted at the end of the unit, the class can see whose estimate came the closest.

New Materials:

- **Books**

  Henri Matisse: Drawing with Scissors by Jane O'Connor (Grosset & Dunlap, 2002)

Suggested Activities with New and Existing Materials:

Students can…

- make a sculpture of a form of transportation from recyclables.

- draw and paint pictures of forms of transportation. Each student should choose on form of transportation. Encourage students to show lots of background details. Encourage students to use the reference materials in the center.

Problem-Solving

If your centers are not as productive as you would like them to be you might consider asking yourself the following questions:

Are the activities interesting and challenging?
If most of the students are not working well together, if they are wandering around, if they begin seeking other things to do, or if they consistently indicate they don't want to go to one particular center, then the activities may not be very interesting or challenging. Children will begin doing anything other than the planned activities if the activities don't engage them.

When did I last change the center activities?
Children may like the activities you have planned, but that will only last for a certain period of time. Changing the materials and activities keeps the centers fresh and the children engaged.

Do children need/want more choice and control?
If children complete what you have planned in short periods of time, or if they begin to elaborate on your plans, they may be letting you know they are ready to be "in charge" of their own learning. Consider placing some more open-ended activities in the centers and see what happens.

Are the centers tied to classroom themes and other curriculum areas?
Children are more likely to be engaged in activities that are related to themes they are studying in class. This allows children to manipulate and expand upon the concepts being learned. If students don't seem to be engaged in center activities, check to see if there are enough connections to the other things you are doing during the day.

Are students ready (and am I ready) to introduce projects as a part of my centers?
Projects tend to be more in-depth studies of a topic with students engaging in a chosen study for a period of time (one or more weeks depending on the topic). There are identified stages of project development: topic identification, discussion, fieldwork, representation, investigation, and display. If students appear to be interested in a given topic or want to be engaged in an investigation of one concept, you may want to consider allowing them to spend several days working on it. For more information, see:

Engaging Children's Minds: The Project Approach by L. G. Katz and S. C. Chard (Ablex, 2000)

Additional Ideas and Materials

Reading | Writing | Home Living | Community | Blocks | Science | Math | Art

December and January Special Reading Place—Igloo

Materials:

- **200 Empty Plastic Gallon (4 L) Jugs**

   If you use milk jugs, be sure to rinse them well. It is a good idea to save the lids (if possible) and glue them onto the jugs before making the igloo.

- **Hot Glue Gun and Glue**

   This is a teacher project.

   Lay 20 jugs, bottoms facing out, in a circle on the floor. Remove four or five of the jugs to create a doorway. Use hot glue to attach each jug to the adjacent jugs. Be careful not to touch the plastic jugs with the metal tip of the glue gun.

   Glue a row of jugs on top of the bottom row, being sure to attach the jugs on the bottoms and the sides.

Continue adding rows of jugs until the igloo is five rows high. When gluing the sixth row of jugs, continue attaching until you have a complete circle. This creates a row of jugs over the door and is the start of the roof section.

Continue adding rows of jugs, decreasing the number of jugs in each row to create a dome. When you have room at the top for only one jug, cut one in half. Take the bottom half of the jug and turn it so the opening is pointing down into the igloo. Then, glue the half-jug into place.

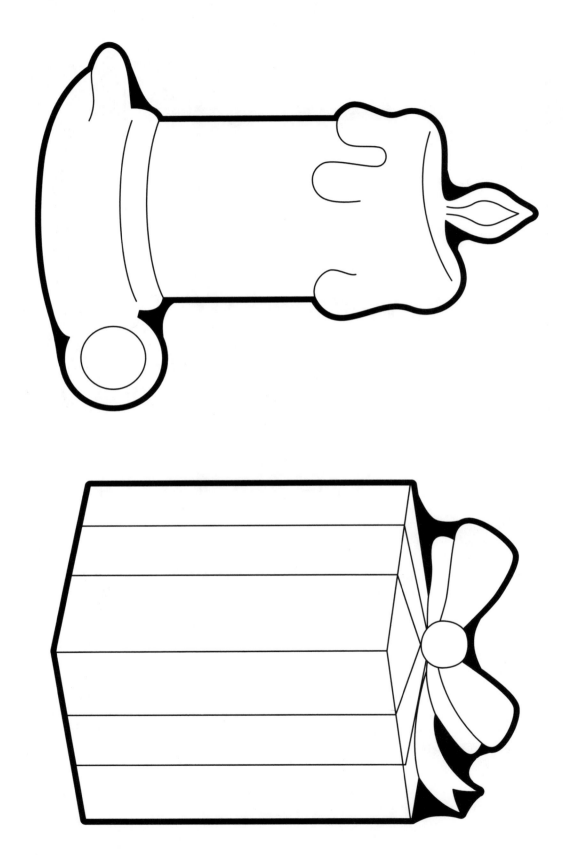

January Shape Book

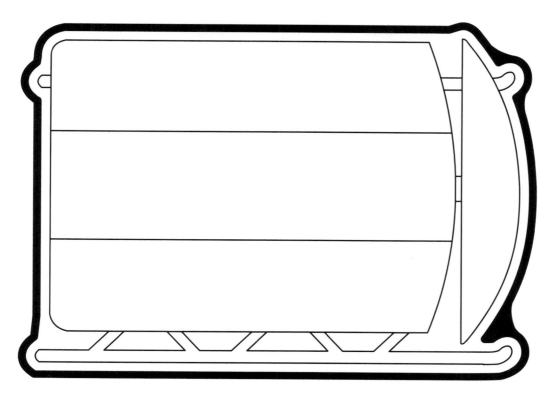

February Shape Book

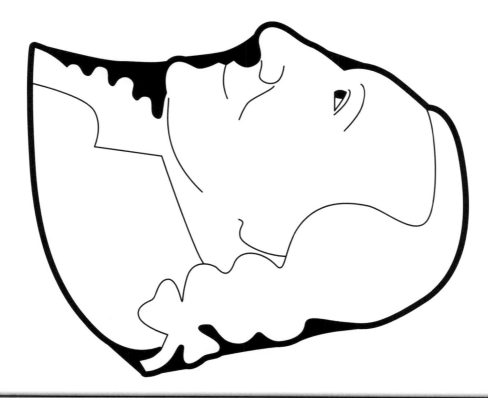

February Shape Book

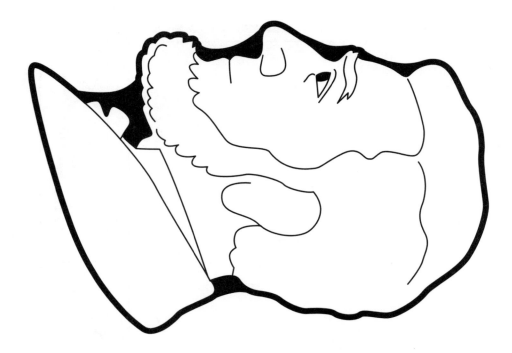

All about Me Shape Book

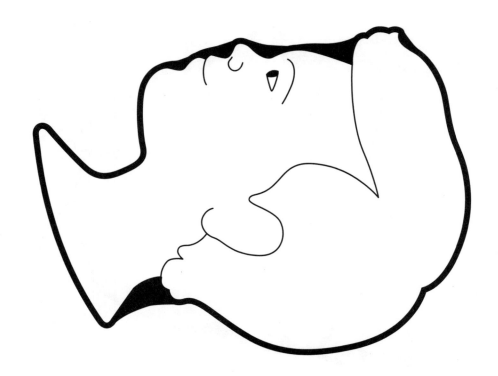

All about Me Shape Book

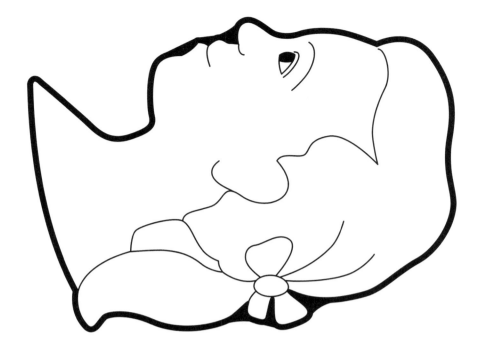

Friends Shape Book

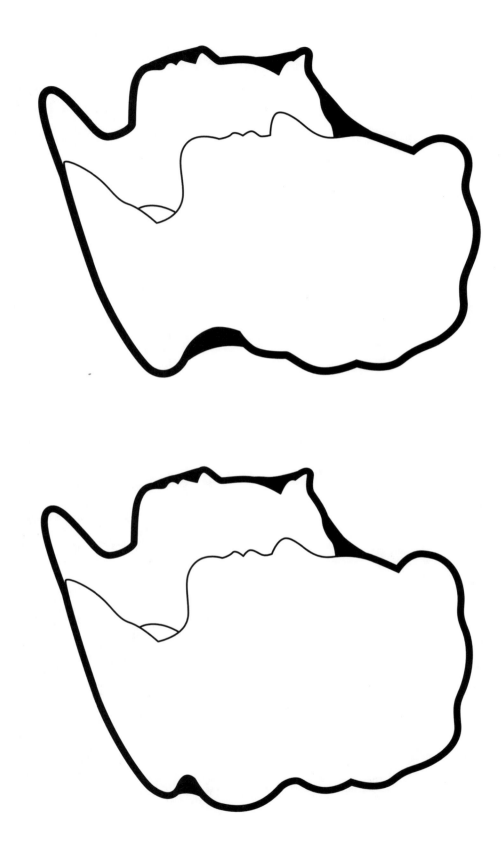

Plants Shape Book/Living and Non-Living Shape Book

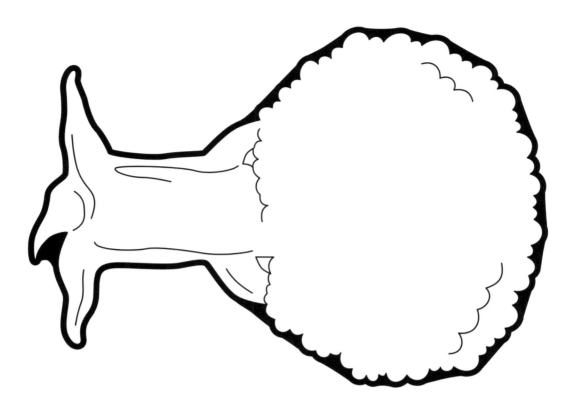

Dinosaur Shape Book

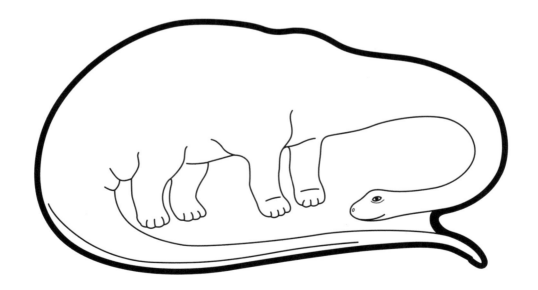

Farm Animal Shape Book

Water Shape Book

Water Shape Book

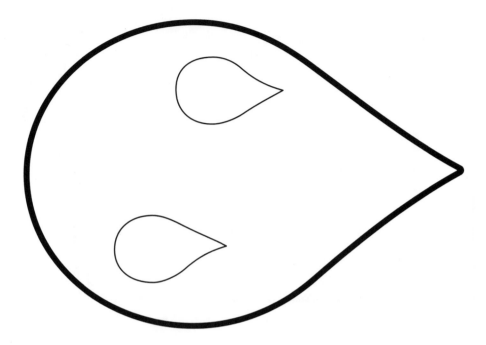

Weather Shape Book

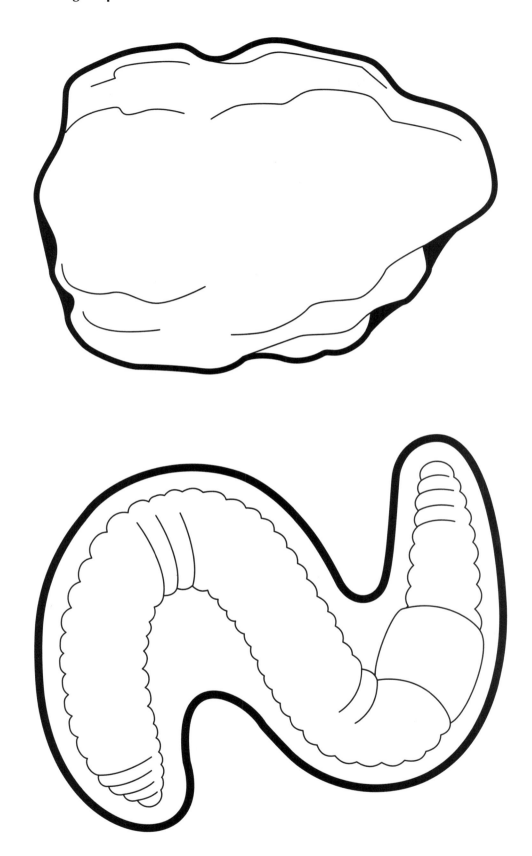

Living and Non-Living Shape Book

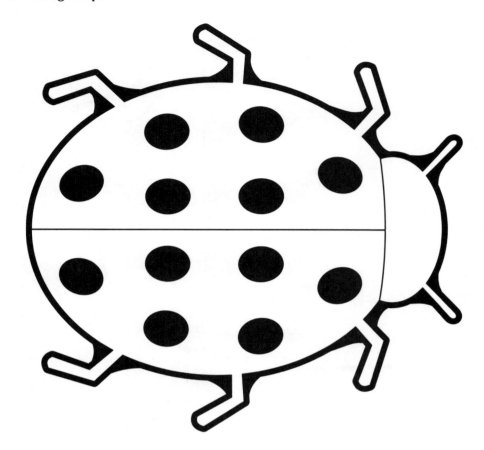

Colors Shape Book

August/September Pattern Cards

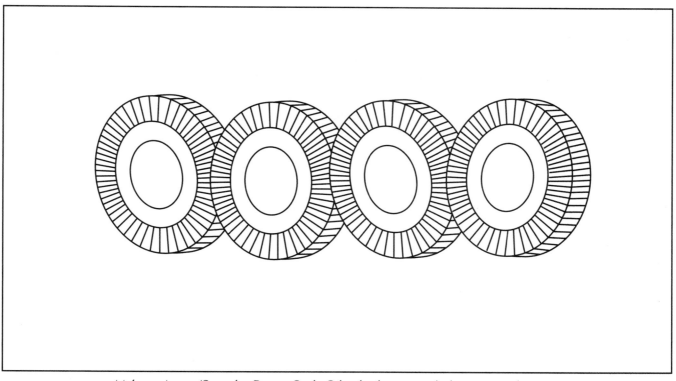

Make 10 August/September Pattern Cards. Color the chips to match chips in your classroom.
Chips should make AB patterns with different colors on each card.

October Pattern Cards

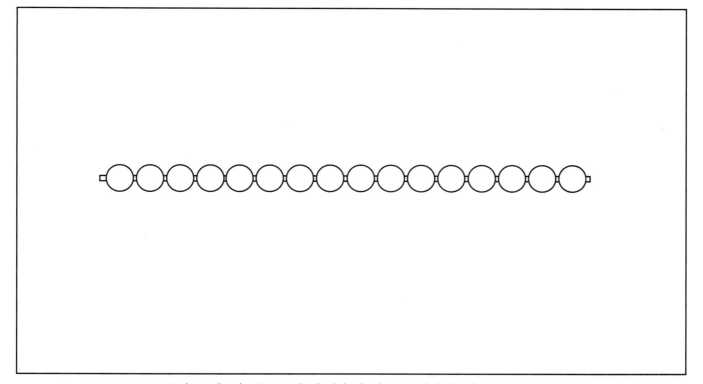

Make 10 October Pattern Cards. Color beads to match the beads in your set.
Beads should make ABC patterns with different colors on each card.

November Pattern Cards

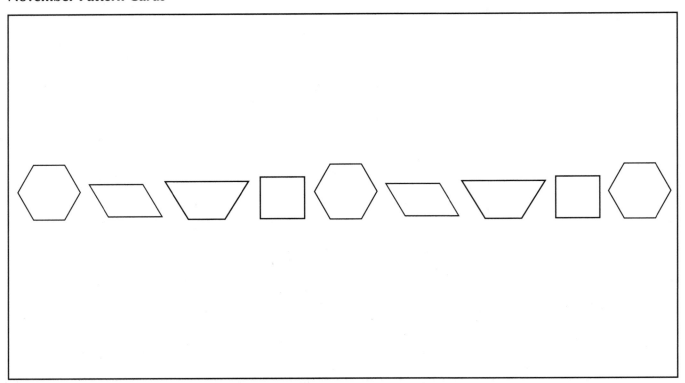

Color the pattern blocks to match the colors of your set.

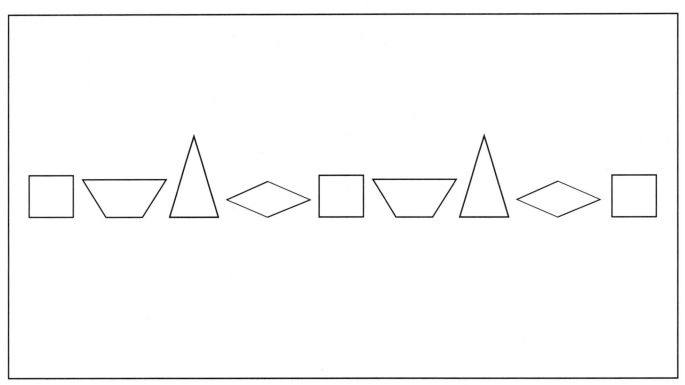

Color the pattern blocks to match the colors of your set.

November Pattern Cards

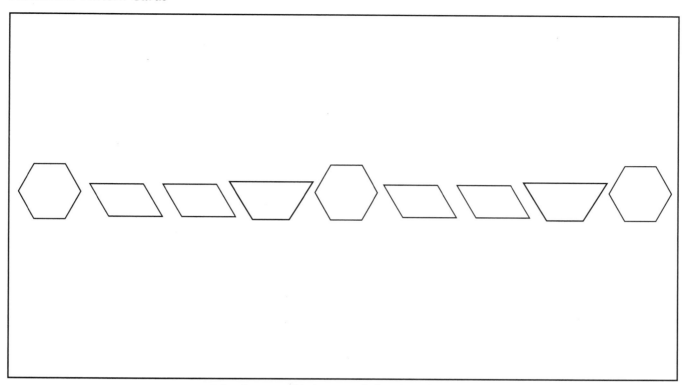

Color the pattern blocks to match the colors of your set.

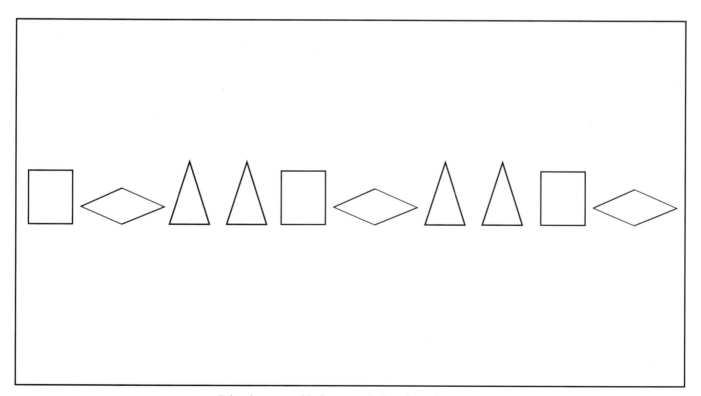

Color the pattern blocks to match the colors of your set.

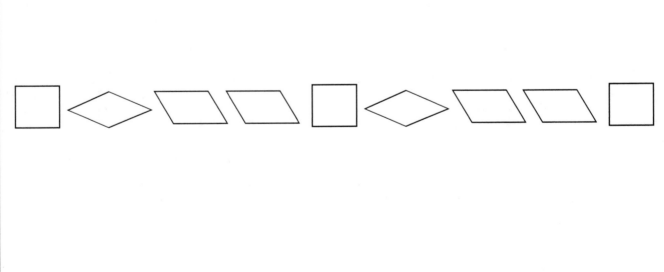

Color the pattern blocks to match the colors of your set.

Color the pattern blocks to match the colors of your set.

November Pattern Cards

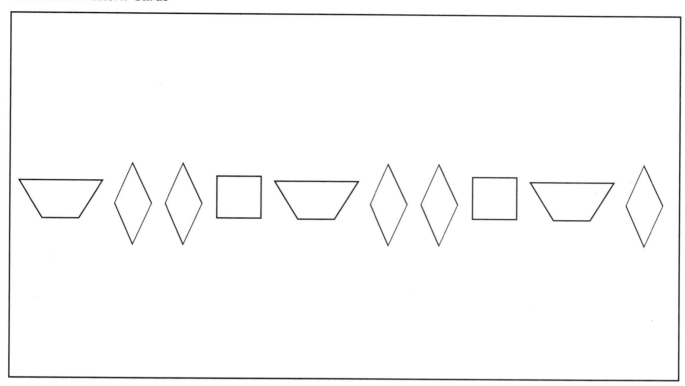

Color the pattern blocks to match the colors of your set.

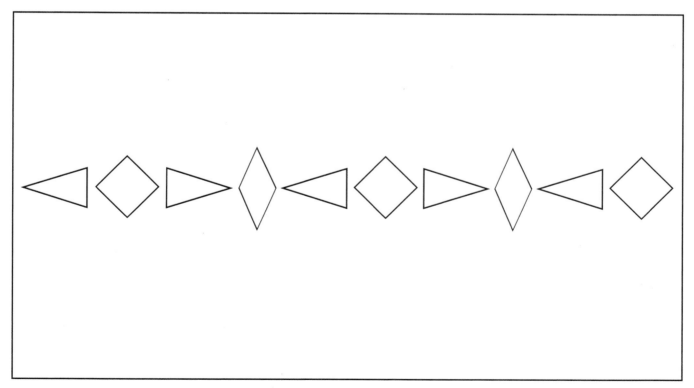

Color the pattern blocks to match the colors of your set.

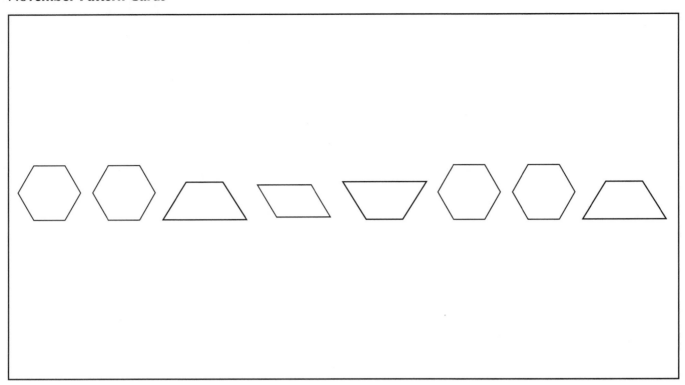

Color the pattern blocks to match the colors of your set.

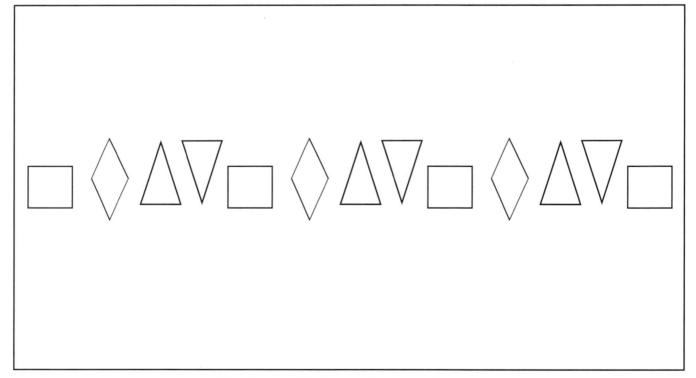

Color the pattern blocks to match the colors of your set.

December Pattern Cards

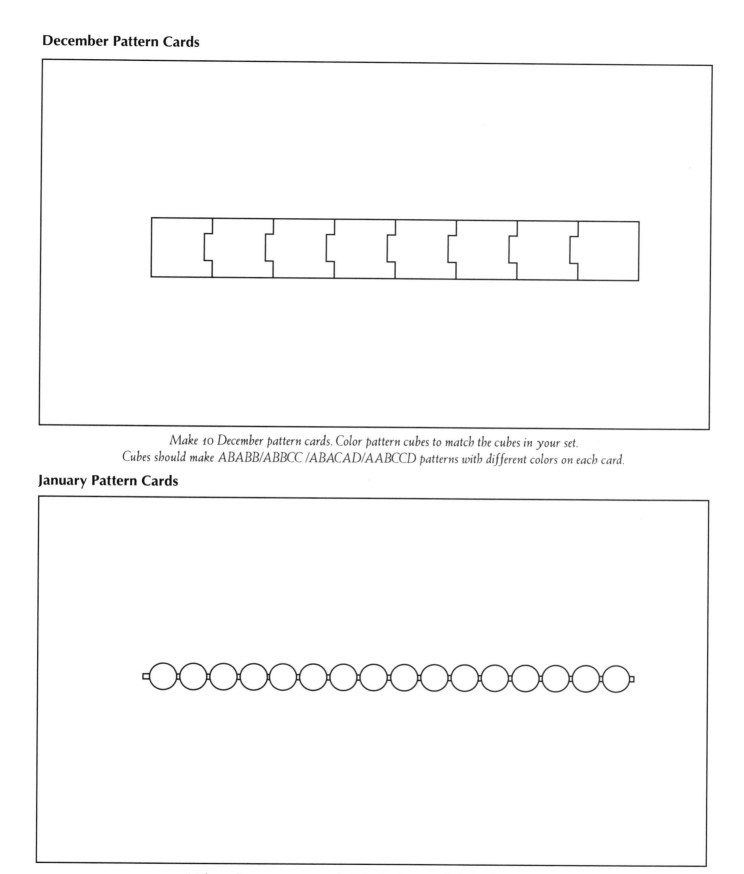

Make 10 December pattern cards. Color pattern cubes to match the cubes in your set.
Cubes should make ABABB/ABBCC /ABACAD/AABCCD patterns with different colors on each card.

January Pattern Cards

Make 10 January pattern cards. Color beads to match the beads in your set.
Beads should make ABABB/ABBAC/AABCB/ABACC/ABCAC patterns with different colors on each card.

February Pattern Cards

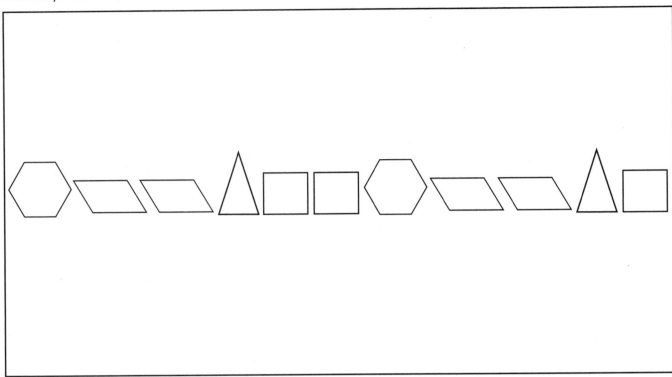

Color the pattern blocks to match the colors of your set.

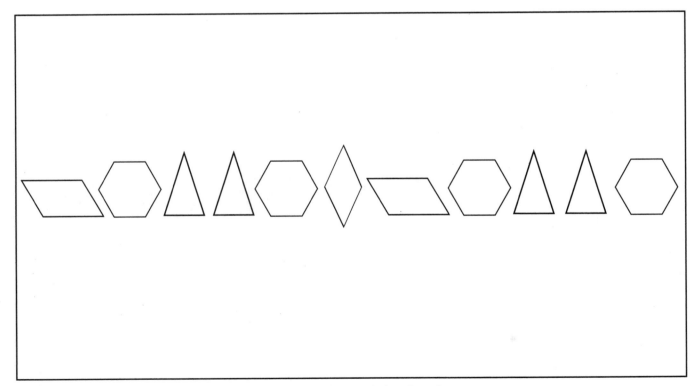

Color the pattern blocks to match the colors of your set.

February Pattern Cards

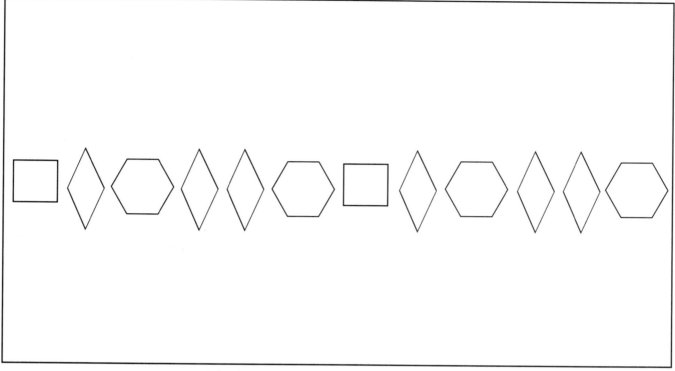

Color the pattern blocks to match the colors of your set.

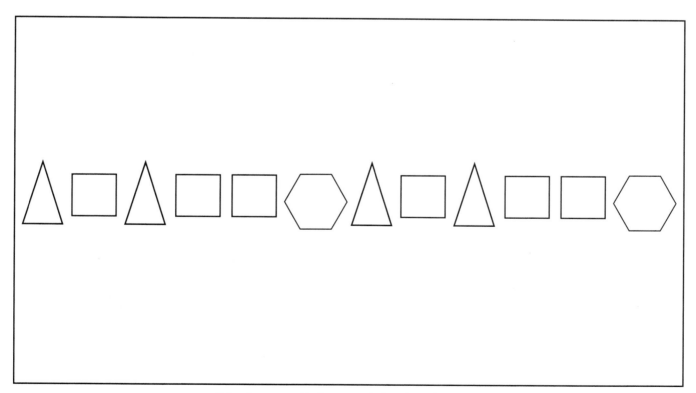

Color the pattern blocks to match the colors of your set.

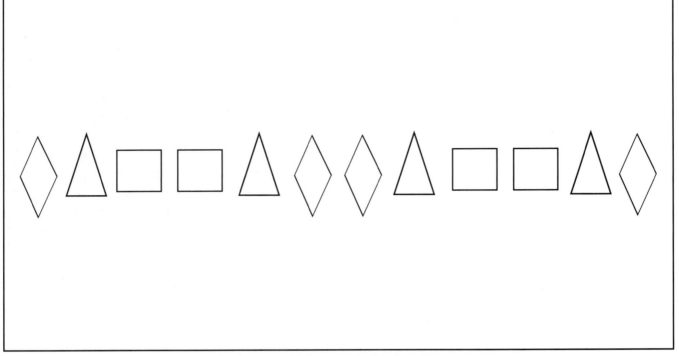

Color the pattern blocks to match the colors of your set.

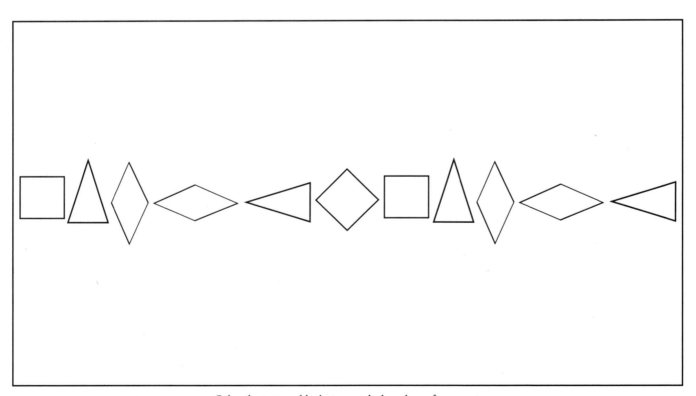

Color the pattern blocks to match the colors of your set.

February Pattern Cards

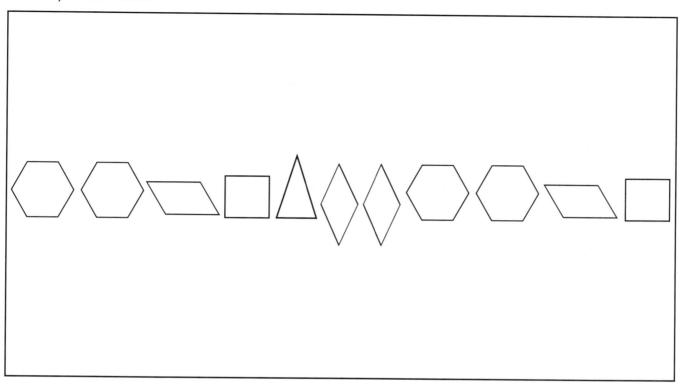

Color the pattern blocks to match the colors of your set.

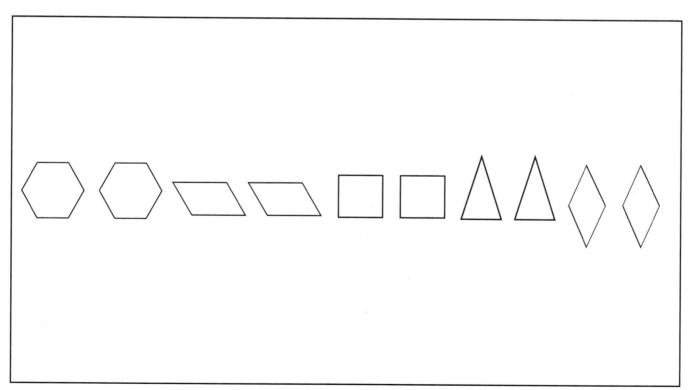

Color the pattern blocks to match the colors of your set.

February Pattern Cards

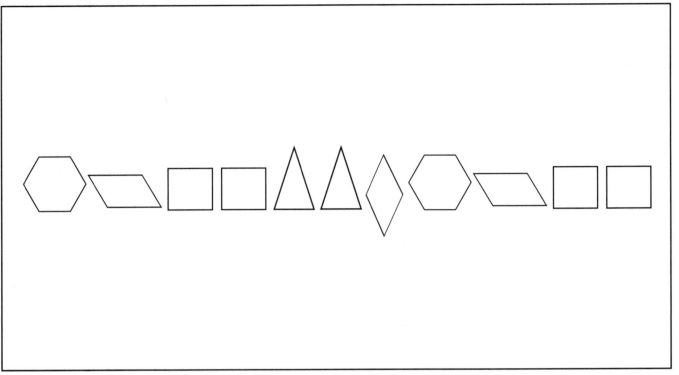

Color the pattern blocks to match the colors of your set.

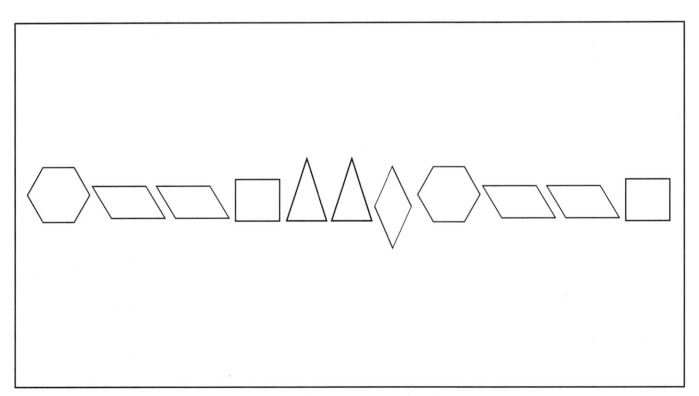

Color the pattern blocks to match the colors of your set.

March Pattern Cards

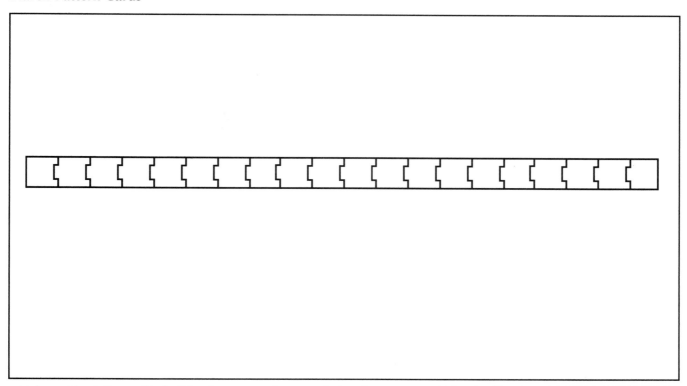

Make ten March Pattern Cards. Color the pattern cubes to match the cubes in your set. Cubes should make AABBCCDDEEFFGGHH/ ABBCDDEFFGHH/ABCDDEEFGH/AABCDEEFGH/ABCCDDEFGGHHIJ patterns with different colors on each card.

References

Reading | Writing | Home Living | Community | Blocks | Science | Math | Art

PROFESSIONAL REFERENCES

Bredekamp, S. (ed.) (1987). *Developmentally Appropriate Practices in Early Childhood Programs Serving Children from Birth through Age 8*. Washington, D.C.: National Association for the Education of Young Children.

Edwards, C. P. (1993). *The Hundred Languages of Children: The Reggio Emilia Approach to Early Childhood Education*. Norwood, NJ: Ablex Publishing Corporation

Funderstanding.com *http://www.funderstanding.com/vygotsky.cfm* retrieved 5-29-02.

Hall, D. P., Arens, A. B., and Loman, K. L. (2002). *The Administrator's Guide to Building Blocks™*. Greensboro, NC: Carson-Dellosa.

Hall, D. P. and Cunningham, P. M. (1997). *Month-by-Month Reading and Writing for Kindergarten*. Greensboro, NC: Carson-Dellosa.

Hall, D. P. and Loman, K.L. (2002). *Interactive Charts: Shared Reading for Kindergarten and First Grade*. Greensboro, NC: Carson-Dellosa.

Hall, D. P. and Williams, E. (2000). *The Teacher's Guide to Building Blocks™*. Greensboro, NC: Carson-Dellosa.

Hall, D. P. and Williams, E. (2001). *Predictable Charts: Shared Writing for Kindergarten and First Grade*. Greensboro, NC: Carson-Dellosa.

Headley, Neith E. (1959) *Foster and Headley's Education in the Kindergarten, Third Edition*. New York, NY: American Book Company.

Katz, L.G. and Chard, S.C. (2000) *Engaging Children's Minds: The Project Approach, Second Edition*. Norwood, NJ: Ablex Publishing Corporation.

Korat, O., Bahar, E., and Snapir, M. (2002). "Sociodramatic Play as Opportunity for Literacy Development: The Teacher's Role." *The Reading Teacher,* 56(4): 386-393.

Neuman, S. and Roskos, K. (1997). "Literacy Knowledge in Practice: Contexts of Participation for Young Writers and Readers." *Reading Research Quarterly,* 32(1): 10-32.

Northwest Regional Educational Laboratory. (1998). *Learning to Read and Write: A Place to Start*. Portland, OR: Northwest Regional Educational Laboratory.

Owocki, G. (1999). *Literacy through Play*. Portsmouth, NH: Heinemann.

Singer, D. G. and Reverson, T. A. (1978). *A Piaget Primer: How a Child Thinks*. New York, NY: Plume.

Snow, C.E., Burns, M. A., and Griffin, P. (eds.) (1998). *Preventing Reading Difficulties in Young Children*. Washington, DC: National Academy Press.

CHILDREN'S BOOKS CITED

1-2-3 Draw Dinosaurs and Other Prehistoric Animals by Freddie Levin (Peel Productions, 2001)

1-2-3 Draw Pets and Farm Animals: A Step by Step Guide by Freddie Levin (Peel Productions, 2000)

A Is for Artist: A Getty Museum Alphabet by John Harris (J. Paul Getty Museum Publications, 1997)

The ABC Exhibit by Leonard Fisher (Atheneum, 1991)

ABC I Like Me! by Nancy Carlson (Puffin Books, 1999)

ABC T-Rex by Bernard Most (Harcourt, 2000)

The Adventures of a Nose by Viviane Schwartz (Candlewick Press, 2002)

Airport by Byron Barton (HarperTrophy, 1987)

All Aboard ABC by Doug Magee and Robert Newman (Cobblehill, 1990)

All Aboard Trains by Mary Harding (Grosset & Dunlap, 1989)

All About Owls by Jim Arnosky (Scholastic, Inc., 1999)

Alpha Bugs: A Pop-Up Alphabet by David Carter (Little Simon, 1994)

Alphabears: An ABC Book by Kathleen Hague (Henry Holt and Company, Inc., 1999)

Alphabet Adventure by Audrey Wood (Blue Sky Press, 2001)

The Alphabet Book by P. D. Eastman (Random House, 1974)

Alphabet City by Stephen T. Johnson (Puffin Books, 1999)

Alphabet Soup: A Feast of Letters by Scott Gustafson (The Greenwich Workshop Press, 1994)

The Alphabet Tree by Leo Lionni (Knopf, 1990)

And to Think That We Thought That We'd Never Be Friends by Mary Ann Hoberman (Dragonfly, 2003)

Animal ABC by David Wojtowycz (Sterling, 2000)

Annabelle Swift, Kindergartner by Amy Schwartz (Orchard Books, 1991)

Anno's Counting Book by Mitsumasa Anno (HarperTrophy, 1986)

Antics!: An Alphabetical Anthology by Cathi Hepworth (Puffin Books, 1996)

Ape in a Cape: An Alphabet of Odd Animals by Fritz Eichenberg (Voyager Books, 1989)

Are You a Snail? by Judy Allen and Tudor Humphries (Kingfisher, 2000)

Arthur Writes a Story by Marc Brown (Little, Brown and Company, 1996)

Aunt Isabel Tells a Good One by Kate Duke (Puffin Books, 1994)

Autumn: An Alphabet Acrostic by Steven Schnur (Clarion Books, 1997)

Backyard Detective: Critters Up Close by Nic Bishop (Scholastic, Inc., 2002)

Barn by Debby Atwell (Houghton Mifflin, 2001)

Barnyard Banter by Denise Fleming (Henry Holt and Company, Inc., 2001)

Bartholomew and the Oobleck by Dr. Seuss (Random House, 1970)

The Baseball Counting Book by Barbara McGrath (Charlesbridge Publishing, 1999)

Beach Day by Karen Roosa (Clarion Books, 2001)

Bear at Home by Stella Blackstone (Barefoot Books, 2001)

The Berenstain Bears and the Trouble with Friends by Stan and Jan Berenstain (Random House, 1987)

The Berenstain Bears Go to Camp by Stan and Jan Berenstain (Random House, 1982)

Best Friends for Frances by Russell Hoban (HarperTrophy, 1976)

Best Friends by Steven Kellogg (Puffin Books, 1992)

The Big Orange Splot by Daniel Pinkwater (Scholastic, Inc., 1993)

Big Pumpkin by Erica Silverman (Aladdin Library, 1995)

Big Red Barn by Margaret Wise Brown (HarperCollins, 1989)

The Big Red Bus by Judy Hindley (Candlewick Press, 2000)

The Big Wide-Mouthed Frog: A Traditional Tale by Ana Larranaga (Candlewick Press, 1999)

Birds by Brian Wildsmith (Oxford Press, 1980)

Birdsong by Audrey Wood (Voyager Books, 2001)

Block City by Robert Louis Stevenson (Puffin Books, 1992)

A Book of Letters by Ken Wilson-Max (Cartwheel Books, 2002)

Bridges Are to Cross by Philemon Sturges (Puffin Books, 2000)

Bridges Connect: A Building Block Book by Lee Sullivan Hill (Carolrhoda Books, 1996)

Bugs! Bugs! Bugs! by Bob Barner (Chronicle Books, 1999)

Building a House by Byron Barton (William Morrow, 1981)

The Butterfly Alphabet by Kjell Sandved (Scholastic, Inc., 1999)

Can I Have a Stegosaurus, Mom? Can I? Please!? by Lois Grambling (Troll, 1998)

Can I Keep Him? by Steven Kellogg (Puffin Books, 1992)

Caps, Hats, Socks and Mittens: A Book About the Four Seasons by Louise Borden (Scholastic, Inc., 1992)

Car Wash by Sandra Steen and Susan Steen (Puffin Books, 2003)

Carl's Christmas by Alexandra Day (Farrar, Straus & Giroux, 1994)

The Carrot Seed by Ruth Krauss (HarperTrophy, 1989)

Cars by Anne Rockwell (Puffin Books, 1992)

Castle by David MacAulay (Houghton Mifflin/Walter Lorraine Books, 1982)

Cathedral: The Story of Its Construction by David MacAulay (Houghton Mifflin/Walter Lorraine Books, 1981)

Cats, Cats, Cats! by Leslea Newman (Simon & Schuster, Inc., 2001)

Chicka Chicka Boom Boom by John Archambault (Aladdin Library, 2000)

The Chick and the Duckling by Mirra Ginsburg (Aladdin Library, 1988)

A Child's Book of Art: Discover Great Paintings by Lucy Micklethwait (Dorling Kindersley Publishing, 1999)

City: A Story of Roman Planning and Construction by David MacAulay (Houghton Mifflin/Walter Lorraine Books, 1983)

Claude Monet: Sunshine and Waterlilies by True Kelley (Grossett & Dunlap, 2001)

The Cloud Book by Tomie De Paola (Holiday House, 1985)

Click, Clack, Moo: Cows That Type by Doreen Cronin (Simon & Schuster, Inc., 2000)

Clifford, the Big Red Dog by Norman Bridwell (Scholastic, Inc., 1985)

Climbing Tree Frogs by Ruth Berman (Lerner Publications Company, 1998)

Cloud Dance by Thomas Locker (Voyager Books, 2003)

Cloudy with a Chance of Meatballs by Judi Barrett (Aladdin Library, 1982)

The Clubhouse by Anastasia Suen (Puffin, 2003)

Color by Ruth Heller (Puffin Books, 1999)

A Color of His Own by Leo Lionni (Dragonfly, 1997)

Come On, Rain! by Karen Hesse (Scholastic, Inc., 1999)

Cool Ali by Nancy Poydar (Margaret K. McElderry Books, 1996)

Country Crossing by Jim Aylesworth (Aladdin Library, 1995)

Cranberry Thanksgiving by Wende and Harry Devlin (Scott Foresman, 1990)

Dear Mr. Blueberry by Simon James (Aladdin Library, 1996)

Dinosaur Bones by Bob Barner (Chronicle Books, 2001)

Dinosaur Roar! by Paul and Henrietta Stickland (Puffin Books, 2002)

Dinosaur Stomp!: A Monster Pop-Up Book by Paul Stickland (Dutton Books, 1996)

Dinosaurs, Dinosaurs by Byron Barton (Harpercollins Juvenile Books, 1991)

Dogs, Dogs, Dogs! by Leslea Newman (Simon & Schuster, Inc., 2002)

Don't Need Friends by Carolyn Crimi (Dragonfly, 2001)

Down by the Cool of the Pool by Tony Mitton (The Watts Publishing Group, 2002)

Eating the Alphabet: Fruits and Vegetables from A to Z by Lois Ehlert (Voyager Books, 1993)

Ed Emberley's Drawing Book of Animals by Ed Emberley (Little, Brown and Company, 1994)

Ed Emberley's Drawing Book of Faces by Ed Emberley (Little, Brown and Company, 1992)

Edgar Degas: Paintings That Dance by Maryann Cocca-Leffler (Grossett & Dunlap, 2001)

Edward the Emu by Sheena Knowles (HarperTrophy, 1998)

The Emperor's Egg by Martin Jenkins (Candlewick Press, 2002)

Eric Carle's Animals Animals by Eric Carle (Puffin Books, 1999)

Everybody Needs a Rock by Byrd Baylor (Scott Foresman, 1985)

Eyes, Nose, Fingers, and Toes by Judy Hindley (Candlewick Press, 2002)

Families by Ann Morris (HarperCollins, 2000)

Family by Isabell Monk (Lerner Publications Company, 2001)

Farm Animals, Eye Openers by Angela Royston (Penguin Books, Ltd., 1999)

Farmer Brown Goes Round and Round by Teri Sloat (Dorling Kindersley Publishing, 2001)

Feast for Ten by Cathryn Falwell (Clarion Books, 1995)

Feathers for Lunch by Lois Ehlert (Voyager Books, 1996)

Figuring Figures by Brigitte Baumbusch (House of Stratus, 2002)

First Day Jitters by Julie Danneberg (Charlesbridge Publishing, 2000)

First Day, Hooray! by Nancy Poydar (Holiday House, 2000)

The First Starry Night by Joan Shaddox Isom (Whispering Coyote Press, 2001)

Fish Eyes by Lois Ehlert (Voyager Books, 1992)

Five Little Monkeys Jumping on the Bed by Eileen Christelow (Scott Foresman, 1989)

Five Little Pumpkins by Iris Van Rynbach (Boyds Mills Press, 2003)

Flower Garden by Eve Bunting (Voyager Books, 2000)

The Foot Book by Dr. Seuss (Random House, 1968)

Freight Train by Donald Crews (HarperTrophy, 1992)

Friends by Helme Heine (Aladdin Library, 1997)

Froggy Goes to School by Jonathan London (Puffin Books, 1998)

Froggy's First Kiss by Jonathan London (Puffin Books, 1999)

From Pictures to Words: A Book About Making a Book by Janet Stevens (Holiday House, 1999)

From Seed to Plant by Gail Gibbons (Holiday House, 1993)

Frozen Noses by Jan Carr (Holiday House, 1999)

George and Martha: The Complete Stories of Two Best Friends by James Marshall (Houghton Mifflin, 1997)

Gilberto and the Wind by Marie Hall Ets (Puffin Books, 1978)

Goldilocks and the Three Bears by Jan Brett (Puffin Books, 1996)

Good Dog, Carl by Alexandra Day (Aladdin Library, 1997)

Grandfather and I by Helen Buckley (Harpercollins Juvenile Books, 2000)

The Graphic Alphabet by David Pelletier (Orchard Books, 1996)

Gray Rabbit's 1, 2, 3 by Alan Baker (Larousse Kingfisher Chambers, 1999)

Green Eggs and Ham by Dr. Seuss (Random House, 1960)

The Grouchy Ladybug by Eric Carle (HarperTrophy, 1996)

Growing Vegetable Soup by Lois Ehlert (Voyager Books, 1990)

Guess How Much I Love You? by Sam McBratney (Candlewick Press, 1995)

Halloween by Miriam Nerlove (Albert Whitman & Company, 1989)

The Hallo-Wiener by Dav Pilkey (Scholastic, Inc., 1999)

Hamsters and Gerbils by Ann Larkin Hansen (Checkerboard Library, 1997)

Have You Seen My Duckling? by Nancy Tafuri (HarperTrophy, 1991)

Henri Matisse: Drawing with Scissors by Jane O'Connor (Grosset & Dunlap, 2002)

Hey Little Ant by Phillip and Hannah Hoose (Tricycle Press, 1998)

Horse in the Pigpen by Linda Williams (HarperCollins, 2002)

A House for Hermit Crab by Eric Carle (Aladdin Library, 2002)

Houses and Homes by Ann Morris (HarperTrophy, 1995)

How a Book Is Made by Aliki (HarperTrophy, 1988)

How Artists See Animals by Colleen Carroll (Abbeville Press, Inc., 1999)

How Artists See Families by Colleen Carroll (Abbeville Press, Inc., 2000)

How Artists See People by Colleen Carroll (Abbeville Press, Inc., 1996)

How Artists See the Weather by Colleen Carroll (Abbeville Press, Inc., 1998)

How Do Dinosaurs Say Good Night? by Jane Yolen (Blue Sky Press, 2000)

How Does the Wind Walk? by Nancy White Carlstrom (Simon & Schuster, Inc., 1993)

How Many Bugs in a Box? by David A. Carter (Little Simon, 1988)

How to Lose All Your Friends by Nancy Carlson (Puffin Books, 1997)

The Hungry Thing by Jan Slepian and Ann Seidler (Scholastic, Inc., 2001)

The Hungry Thing Goes to a Restaurant by Jan Slepian and Ann Seidler (Scholastic, Inc., 1993)

The Hungry Thing Returns by Jan Slepian and Ann Seidler (Scholastic, Inc., 1993)

I Know an Old Lady Who Swallowed a Pie by Alison Jackson (Puffin Books, 2002)

I Love Trains! by Philemon Sturges (HarperTrophy, 2003)

I Love You, Little One by Nancy Tafuri (Cartwheel Books, 2000)

I Met a Bear by Dan Yaccarino (HarperFestival, 2002)

I Spy Two Eyes: Numbers in Art by Lucy Micklethwait (Mulberry Books, 1998)

I Spy: An Alphabet in Art by Lucy Micklethwait (HarperTrophy, 1996)

I Started School Today by Karen G. Frandsen (Children's Book Press, 1994)

I Took a Walk by Henry Cole (Greenwillow Books, 1998)

I Wonder Why by Lois Rock (Chronicle Books, 2001)

The Icky Sticky Frog by Dawn Bentley (Piggy Toes Press, 2001)

If I Were the Wind by Lezlie Evans (Eager Minds Press, 2001)

If You Give a Mouse a Cookie by Laura Joffe Numeroff (HarperTrophy, 1997)

If You Take a Mouse to School by Laura Numeroff (Laura Geringer Books, 2002)

I'll Always Love You by Hans Wilhelm (Crown Publishing Group, 1989)

In November by Cynthia Rylant (Harcourt, 2000)

In the Small, Small Pond by Denise Fleming (Henry Holt and Company, Inc., 1998)

Inch by Inch by Leo Lionni (HarperTrophy, 1995)

Insectlopedia: Poems and Paintings by Douglas Florian (Voyager Books, 2002)

An Island in the Sun by Stella Blackstone (Barefoot Books, 2003)

Is the Sky Always Blue? by Eric Adler (Kansas City Star Books, 2002)

Is Your Mama a Llama? by Deborah Guarino (Scholastic, Inc., 1991)

It Could Still Be a Rock by Allan Fowler (Children's Book Press, 1993)

It Could Still Be Water by Allan Fowler (Children's Book Press, 1993)

It's Pumpkin Time by Zoe Hall (Scholastic, Inc., 1999)

The Jacket I Wear in the Snow by Shirley Neitzel (HarperTrophy, 1994)

Jack's Garden by Henry Cole (Scott Foresman, 1995)

Jamberry by Bruce Degen (HarperTrophy, 1985)

Johnny Appleseed by Steven Kellogg (Harpercollins Juvenile Books, 1996)

The Jolly Christmas Postman by Janet and Allan Ahlberg (Little, Brown and Company, 2001)

The Jolly Postman: Or Other People's Letters by Janet and Allan Ahlberg (Little, Brown and Company, 2001)

Jump, Frog, Jump by Robert Kalan (HarperTrophy, 1989)

Just Like Dad by Gina and Mercer Mayer (Golden Books Publishing Company, Inc., 1998)

Just Me and My Little Brother by Mercer Mayer (Golden Books Publishing Company, Inc., 1998)

Just Me and My Mom by Mercer Mayer (Golden Books Publishing Company, Inc., 2001)

The Kissing Hand by Audrey Penn (Child Welfare League of America, 1993)

Kite Flying by Grace Lin (Random House, 2002)

Ladybug, Ladybug by Ruth Brown (Puffin Books, 1992)

A Light in the Attic by Shel Silverstein (HarperCollins, 1981)

Light the Lights!: A Story About Celebrating Hanukkah and Christmas by Margaret Moorman (Scholastic, Inc. 1999)

Lights of Winter: Winter Celebrations Around the World by Heather Conrad (Lightport Books, 2001)

Lisa's Airplane Trip by Anne Gutman and Georg Hallensleben (Knopf, 2001)

Little Green by Keith Baker (Harcourt, 2001)

Little Miss Spider at Sunnypatch School by David Kirk (Scholastic, Inc., 2000)

Little Mouse's Big Valentine by Thacher Hurd (Harpercollins Juvenile Books, 1992)

The Little School Bus by Carol Roth (North South Books, 2002)

Living Things by Judith Holloway (Modern Curriculum Press, 1993)

Lizards, Frogs, and Polliwogs by Douglas Florian (Harcourt, 2001)

Look Out Kindergarten Here I Come! by Nancy Carlson (Puffin Books, 1999)

Looking at Faces in Art by Joy Richardson (Gareth Stevens, 2000)

Looking at Nature by Brigitte Baumbusch (Stewart, Tabori & Chang, 1999)

Louella Mae, She's Run Away! by Karen Beaumont Alarcon (Henry Holt and Company, Inc., 2002)

Maisy's ABC by Lucy Cousins (Candlewick Press, 1995)

Maisy's Pool by Lucy Cousins (Candlewick Press, 1999)

Mammalabilia by Douglas Florian (Harcourt, 2000)

Marshmallow Kisses by Linda Crotta Brennan (Houghton Mifflin, 2000)

Mary Wore Her Red Dress and Henry Wore His Green Sneakers by Merle Peek (Houghton Mifflin, 1998)

The Milk Makers by Gail Gibbons (Aladdin Library, 1987)

The Mysterious Tadpole by Steven Kellogg (Puffin Books, 1992)

Milly and Tilly: The Story of a Town Mouse and a Country Mouse by Kate Summers (Puffin Books, 2000)

Miss Bindergarten Gets Ready for Kindergarten by Joseph Slate (Puffin Books, 2001)

Miss Nelson Is Missing! by Harry Allard (Houghton Mifflin, 1985)

Miss Spider's ABC by David Kirk (Callaway Editions, 1998)

Miss Spider's Tea Party by David Kirk (Scholastic, Inc., 1994)

The Mitten by Alvin Tresselt (HarperTrophy, 1989)

The Mitten: A Ukrainian Folktale by Jan Brett (Scholastic, Inc., 1990)

The Mixed-Up Chameleon by Eric Carle (HarperTrophy, 1988)

More Parts by Tedd Arnold (Dial Books for Young Readers, 2001)

Mouse Paint by Ellen Stoll Walsh (Voyager Books, 1995)

Mouse's First Valentine by Lauren Thompson (Simon & Schuster, Inc., 2002)

Mrs. McTats and Her Houseful of Cats by Alyssa Satin Capucilli (Margaret K. McElderry Books, 2001)

My Beastie Book of ABC by David Frampton (HarperCollins, 2002)

My Dad Is Awesome by Nick Butterworth (Candlewick Press, 1992)

My Dog Rosie by Isabelle Harper (Scholastic, Inc., 1999)

My Duck by Tanya Linch (Bloomsbury Publishing, 2001)

My Feet by Aliki (Harpercollins Juvenile Books, 1992)

My Five Senses by Aliki (HarperCollins, 1989)

My Hands by Aliki (Harpercollins Juvenile Books, 1992)

My House by Lisa Desimini (Owlet, 1997)

My Many Colored Days by Dr. Seuss (Knopf, 1998)

My Teacher Sleeps in School by Leatie Weiss (Puffin Books, 1985)

My Two Grandmothers by Effin Older (Harcourt, 2000)

My Working Mom by Peter Glassman (HarperTrophy, 1994)

The New Baby by Mercer Mayer (Golden Books Publishing Company, Inc., 2001)

New Road! by Gail Gibbons (Harpercollins Juvenile Books, 1983)

Next Stop Grand Central by Maira Kalman (Puffin Books, 2001)

No More Water in the Tub! by Tedd Arnold (Puffin Books, 2002)

Nora's Room by Jessica Harper (HarperCollins, 2001)

North Country Spring by Reeve Lindbergh (Houghton Mifflin, 1997)

Of Colors and Things by Tana Hoban (HarperTrophy, 1996)

Oh, the Places You'll Go! by Dr. Seuss (Random House, 1990)

Old MacDonald Had a Farm by Carol Jones (Houghton Mifflin, 1998)

The Old Man's Mitten: A Ukrainian Tale retold by Yevonne Pollock (Mondo Publishing, 1995)

Olivia by Ian Falconer (Atheneum, 2000)

On Grandpa's Farm by Vivian Sathre (Houghton Mifflin, 1997)

On Mother's Lap by Ann Herbert Scott (Clarion Books, 1992)

On the Day You Were Born by Debra Frasier (Harcourt, 1995)

On the Go by Ann Morris (HarperTrophy, 1994)

One Duck Stuck by Phyllis Root (Candlewick Press, 2003)

One Frog Too Many by Mercer Mayer (Puffin Books, 1992)

One Gray Mouse by Katherine Burton (Kids Can Press, 2002)

One Little Mouse by Dori Chaconas (Viking Children's Books, 2002)

One Tough Turkey by Steven Kroll (Holiday House, 1982)

One Very Best Valentine's Day by Joan W. Blos (Aladdin Library, 1998)

Our Animal Friends at Maple Hill Farm by Alice and Martin Provensen (Aladdin Library, 2001)

The Perfect Pet by Carol Chataway (Kids Can Press, 2002)

Peter's Chair by Ezra Jack Keats (Puffin Books, 1998)

Picky Mrs. Pickle by Christine M. Schneider (Walker & Company, 2001)

Picture a Letter by Brad Sneed (Phyllis Fogelman Books, 2002)

Pigs by Gail Gibbons (Holiday House, 2000)

The Piggy in the Puddle by Charlotte Pomerantz (Aladdin Library, 1989)

A Pill Bug's Life by John Himmelman (Children's Book Press, 2000)

Planes by Anne Rockwell (Puffin Books, 1993)

Planting a Rainbow by Lois Ehlert (Voyager Books, 1992)

The Post Office Book: Mail and How It Moves by Gail Gibbons (HarperTrophy, 1986)

A Pup Just for Me/A Boy Just for Me by Dorothea P. Seeber (Puffin Books, 2002)

Rain Rain Rivers by Uri Shulevitz (Farrar, Straus and Giroux, 1988)

Rain Song by Lezlie Evans (Houghton Mifflin, 1997)

Rain by Manya Stojic (Chrysalis Books, 2000)

Rain by Robert Kalan (HarperTrophy, 1991)

The Reason for a Flower by Ruth Heller (Puffin Books, 1999)

Red Leaf, Yellow Leaf by Lois Ehlert (Harcourt Children's Books, 1991)

Red Rubber Boot Day by Mary Lyn Ray (Harcourt, 2000)

The Relatives Came by Cynthia Rylant (Pearson Learning, 1993)

Richard Scarry's Cars and Trucks and Things That Go by Richard Scarry (Van Nostrand Reinhold, 1974)

Robin's Room by Margaret Wise Brown (Hyperion Press, 2002)

Rocks in His Head by Carol Otis Hurst (Greenwillow Books, 2001)

The Rose in My Garden by Arnold Lobel (HarperTrophy, 1993)

Roses Are Pink, Your Feet Really Stink by Diane De Groat (HarperTrophy, 1997)

Rosie: A Visiting Dog's Story by Stephanie Calmenson (Houghton Mifflin, 1998)

Rosie's Walk by Pat Hutchins (Scott Foresman, 1971)

Round Trip by Ann Jonas (HarperTrophy, 1990)

Roxaboxen by Barbara Cooney (HarperCollins, 1991)

A Salamander's Life by John Himmelman (Children's Book Press, 1998)

Sally Goes to the Beach by Stephen Huneck (Harry N. Abrams, Inc., 2000)

Sally Goes to the Farm by Stephen Huneck (Harry N. Abrams, Inc., 2002)

Saturday Night at the Dinosaur Stomp by Carol Diggery Shields (Candlewick Press, 2002)

School Buses by Dee Ready (Bridgestone Books, 1997)

School by Emily Arnold McCully (Harpercollins Juvenile Books, 1987)

Sheep in a Jeep by Nancy Shaw (Houghton Mifflin, 1997)

Simon's Book by Henrick Drescher (Harpercollins Children's Books, 1983)

Sky Tree: Seeing Science Through Art by Thomas Locker (HarperTrophy, 2001)

Small Cloud by Ariane (Walker & Company, 1996)

Smile a Lot by Nancy Carlson (Carolrhoda Books, 2002)

Snow Dance by Lezlie Evans (Houghton Mifflin, 1997)

Snowballs by Lois Ehlert (Voyager Books, 1999)

The Snowman by Raymond Briggs (Random House, 1987)

The Snowy Day by Ezra Jack Keats (Puffin Books, 1981)

Squeaking of Art: The Mice Go to the Museum by Monica Wellington (Dutton Books, 2000)

St. Patrick's Day in the Morning by Eve Bunting (Clarion Books, 1983)

Stopping by Woods on a Snowy Evening by Robert Frost (Dutton Books, 2001)

The Storm Book by Charlotte Zolotow (HarperTrophy, 1989)

Summer Stinks by Marty Kelley (Zino Press Children's Books, 2001)

Summer: An Alphabet Acrostic by Steven Schnur (Clarion Books, 2001)

Summersaults: Poems & Paintings by Douglas Florian (Greenwillow Books, 2002)

Ten Dogs in the Window: A Countdown Book by Claire Masurel (North South Books, 1997)

Ten Little Dinosaurs by Pattie Schnetzler (Accord Publishing, Ltd., 1996)

Ten Little Ladybugs by Melanie Gerth (Piggy Toes Press, 2001)

Ten Red Apples by Pat Hutchins (Greenwillow Books, 2000)

Ten Sly Piranhas: A Counting Story in Reverse by William Wise (Dial Books, 1993)

Ten Terrible Dinosaurs by Paul Stickland (Puffin Books, 2000)

Ten, Nine, Eight by Molly Garret Bang (HarperTrophy, 1991)

The Three Bears Holiday Rhyme Book by Jane Yolen (Harcourt, 1995)

The Tiny Seed by Eric Carle (Aladdin Library, 2001)

This Is My Body by Mercer Mayer (Golden Books Publishing Company, Inc., 2000)

This Is My Family by Gina and Mercer Mayer (Golden Books Publishing Company, Inc., 1999)

Time to Sleep by Denise Fleming (Henry Holt and Company, Inc., 2001)

Tiptoe into Kindergarten by Jacqueline Rogers (Cartwheel Books, 2003)

Today Is Thanksgiving! by P. K. Hallinan (Ideals Children Books, 2001)

Toes Have Wiggles, Kids Have Giggles by Harriet Ziefert (Putnam Publishing Group, 2002)

Toot and Puddle by Holly Hobbie (Little, Brown and Company, 1997)

Tops & Bottoms by Janet Stevens (Harcourt, 1995)

Trains by Anne Rockwell (Puffin Books, 1993)

Trash Trucks by Daniel Kirk (Putnam Publishing Group, 1997)

A Tree Is Nice by Janice May Udry (HarperTrophy, 1987)

Truck by Donald Crews (HarperTrophy, 1991)

Tuck in the Pool by Martha Weston (Houghton Mifflin, 2000)

'Twas the Night Before Thanksgiving by Dav Pilkey (Orchard Books, 1990)

Twist and Ernest by Laura T. Barnes (Barnesyard Books, Inc., 2000)

Two Little Trains by Margaret Wise Brown (Harpercollins Juvenile Books, 2003)

The Valentine Bears by Eve Bunting (Clarion Books, 1985)

Valentine Mice! by Bethany Roberts (Houghton Mifflin, 2001)

Valentine's Day by Anne Rockwell (HarperTrophy, 2002)

The Very Quiet Cricket by Eric Carle (Philomel Books, 1990)

Water Dance by Thomas Locker (Voyager Books, 2002)

The Water Hole by Graeme Base (Abrams Books for Young Readers, 2001)

We Are Best Friends by Aliki (William Morrow, 1987)

What Do Authors Do? by Eileen Christelow (Houghton Mifflin, 1997)

What Makes a Bird a Bird? by May Garelick (Mondo Publishing, 1995)

What Makes a Rainbow? by Betty Ann Schwartz (Intervisual Books, Inc., 2000)

What Pete Ate From A-Z by Maira Kalman (Puffin Books, 2003)

What Will the Weather Be Like? by Paul Rogers (Scholastic Paperbacks, 1992)

Whatever Happened to the Dinosaurs? by Bernard Most (Voyager Books, 1987)

The Wheels on the Bus by Paul O. Zelinsky (Dutton Books, 1990)

When Autumn Comes by Robert Maass (Owlet, 1992)

When Dinosaurs Go to School by Linda Martin (Chronicle Books, 2002)

When the Root Children Wake Up by Audrey Wood (Scholastic, Inc., 2002)

When the Wind Stops by Charlotte Zolotow (HarperTrophy, 1997)

Whistle for Willie by Ezra Jack Keats (Puffin Books, 1977)

Why Is Blue Dog Blue? by George Rodrigue (Stewart, Tabori & Chang, 2002)

Will I Have a Friend? by Miriam Cohen (Aladdin Library, 1989)

William's Doll by Charlotte Zolotow (HarperTrophy, 1985)

Willy's Pictures by Anthony Browne (Candlewick Press, 2000)

The Wind Blew by Pat Hutchins (Aladdin Library, 1993)

The Wind's Garden by Bethany Roberts (Bill Martin Books, 2001)

The Wing On A Flea: A Book About Shapes by Ed Emberley (Little, Brown and Company, 2001)

Winter Lullaby by Barbara Seuling (Voyager Books, 2002)

Worms Wiggle by David Pelham (Little Simon, 1989)

Yo! Yes? by Chris Raschka (Orchard Books, 1998)

CHILDREN'S BOOKS WITH AUDIOTAPES/CDS

The Z Was Zapped: A Play in Twenty-Six Acts by Chris Van Allsburg (Houghton Mifflin, 1998)

Arthur Writes a Story by Marc Brown (Little Brown Audio, 1999)

Chicka Chicka Boom Boom by John Archambault (Simon & Schuster, Inc., 1991)

Clifford, the Big Red Dog by Norman Bridwell (Scholastic Audio Cassette, 1988)

Feast for Ten by Cathryn Falwell (Clarion Books, 1996)

Five Little Monkeys Jumping on the Bed by Eileen Christelow (Clarion Books, 1991)

Freight Train by Donald Crews (William Morrow & Company, 1992)

Green Eggs and Ham by Dr. Seuss (Random House, 1987)

If You Give a Mouse a Cookie by Laura Joffe Numeroff (HarperFestival, 1994)

In the Small, Small Pond by Denise Fleming (Henry Holt and Company, Inc., 1993)

Jamberry by Bruce Degen (HarperFestival, 1998)

A Light in the Attic by Shel Silverstein (Sony Wonder, 1992)

Mary Wore Her Red Dress and Henry Wore His Green Sneakers by Merle Peek (Clarion Books, 1993)

Miss Nelson Is Missing! by Harry Allard (Houghton Mifflin, 1993)

On Mother's Lap by Ann Herbert Scott (Clarion Books, 1994)

On the Day You Were Born by Debra Frasier (Harcourt Young Classics, 1992)

The Reason for a Flower by Ruth Heller (Spoken Arts, 1999)

Rosie's Walk by Pat Hutchins (Weston Woods Studio, 1972)

The Snowy Day by Ezra Jack Keats (Kimbo Educational Audio, 1984)

St. Patrick's Day in the Morning by Eve Bunting (Clarion Books, 2001)

Notes

Reading Writing Home Living Community Blocks Science Math Art